HOPES AND HELPS

FOR

The Young of both Sexes.

RELATING TO

THE FORMATION OF CHARACTER, CHOICE OF AVOCATION, HEALTH, AMUSEMENT, MUSIC, CONVERSATION, CULTIVATION OF INTELLECT, MORAL SENTIMENT, SOCIAL AFFECTION, COURTSHIP, AND MARRIAGE

BY

REV. G. S. WEAVER,

AUTHOR OF "LECTURES ON MENTAL SCIENCE," ETC., ETC.

Wisdom's ways are ways of pleasantness, and all her paths are peace —BIBLE

NEW YORK:
FOWLERS AND WELLS, PUBLISHERS,
CLINTON HALL, 131 NASSAU STREET.
London: 142 Strand.
Boston: 142 Washington St. | 1854. | Philadelphia: 231 Arch Street.

NEW YORK STEREOTYPE ASSOCIATION,
201 William Street.

PREFACE.

THE design of this work is encouragement for the YOUNG. The author's brief experience and observation have taught him that Youth need encouragement, advisedly given, more than any thing else. Every word of hearty cheer is a breath of inspiration to those just entering upon life's solemn duties. Every book breathing trust and hope, mingled with the friendly suggestions of wisdom and experience, is of real value to them. What if they have read others? Another may still be useful. Shall they hear no sermon next Sabbath, because they heard one last? Shall no book on religion be published, because the Bible is in the hands of all?

One book read only prepares the way for another, though it may be on the same subject. The sight of one scene of beauty gives us a taste for another. The formation of one friendship warms the heart for another.

Every writer can write for some minds, and no one can write for all. In hopes that a kindred chord may be struck in the minds of some Youth, which shall awaken them to a higher life, and a deeper realization of their own importance, and the beauty and immense utility of virtuous living, this work is sent out. Go, little book, and as thou dost go, speak of thy mission to the Youth thou dost meet; and the Father's blessing be upon thee!

G. S. W.

ST LOUIS, M)

CONTENTS.

LECTURE I.

INTRODUCTION.

LECTURE II.

MEDITATION.

LECTURE III.

THE DANGERS OF IMPULSE.

LECTURE IV.

FORMATION OF CHARACTER

LECTURE V.

CHOICE OF AVOCATION, AND PERSEVERANCE

LECTURE VI.

HEALTH.

LECTURE VII.

TEMPERANCE.

LECTURE VIII.

AMUSEMENTS.

LECTURE IX.

MUSIC.

LECTURE X.

CHASTITY OF LANGUAGE.

LECTURE XI.

CULTIVATION OF THE INTELLECT.

LECTURE XII.

CULTIVATION OF THE MORAL SENTIMENTS.

LECTURE XIII.

CULTIVATION OF THE AFFECTIONS.

LECTURE XIV.

COURTSHIP.

LECTURE XV.

MARRIAGE.

HOPES AND HELPS.

LECTURE I.

INTRODUCTION.

Responsibility of the Teacher's Mission—Importance of a Single Thought—Facility of the Youthful Mind—Author's Sympathy with the Young—The Sea of Life—Life, a Scene of Progression—Anticipations of the Young—Dangers in Life's Journey—Youthful Fear and Instability—True and False Bravery—Moral Courage—Free Institutions, a Nursery for Youth—Self-made or Never Made—Good and Bad Luck—Youth, the Seed-time of Age—Age, the Harvest Season of Life—The Young, Heirs to the Past and Future—What will you do with the Future?—An Answer demanded—Duties and Rewards of the Young.

No position in the minister's or the author's life is more responsible than that of lecturer or essayist to youth. And if apologies from a mortal are ever needed, they are when such offices are assumed. If a *man* should ever tremble, it should be when he essays to impress convictions upon youthful minds; for in them he will touch chords strung by the Infinite Organist of creation, which will vibrate when he shall be gathered to his fathers, which will echo and re-echo from hill to hill down the valley of life, and reverberate along the shores of eternity. A thought struck into a young mind! Who shall tell what it will bring forth? It may overturn empires, undermine systems, reconstruct states, metamorphose philosophy, and remodel the fabric of society. A single seed-thought in the minds of Luther, Franklin, Gall, and Fulton, led the way to the changes and victories, yea to the wonders with which the world has been startled within the last three hundred years, and which have put a new face upon, and a new heart into, human affairs. It is so with almost every mind, even those whose doings have been all within themselves. A thought has started a new life, established a new earth, and spread a new heaven in the soul. Often in minds unknown to fame there are revolutions not less wonderful and extensive in their influence, than those which suddenly shock and stir the world. The deep river runs still. The silent influences of the calm old sun, are mightier far than the storm-crash or earthquake-shock. Every mind, in the course of its progressive and eternal being, passes through changes that outvie in grandeur and importance the revolutions of the whole world in any one century, and all these may be, and no doubt often are, sensibly affected by a single thought. Better measure the circuit of Orion than think to measure the influence of a thought.

A good thought or a virtuous impression may redeem a whole life from sin and misery; and a bad impression may work a corresponding amount of ruin, with all their secondary and ultimate results, which no human stretch of thought can comprehend.

We stand amid mysteries momentous and grand. The

nerves of the universe of intelligence are strung about us beneath the visible creation, and we touch them, turn which way we will. Every touch from every human creature produces a wide sensation, either pleasant or unpleasant, agreeable or painful, according to the wisdom or folly of the touch, or its virtuous or vicious nature. He who stands in any of the nervous centers of this universal body of intelligence, of course produces the greater sensation according to his position.

These thoughts can not fail to impress us with our personal responsibilities, and ought not to fail to affect duly and deeply him who occupies any position among the instructors of youth.

One may talk to age, and the opinions, and habits, and states of mind held and cherished for years unaltered, will prevent his words from making any impression deeper than that which trembles on the ear-drum.

So he may lecture to manhood in its vigor, and the world will roll its great ball of business, fame, and sin between him and the souls he would reach, and well-nigh drown his words, though they may be pregnant with wisdom and love. But the ear of youth is open, and ready to catch every sound, and to be impressed with every thought.

This adds additional responsibility to the adviser of youth, but at the same time urges him on to nobler efforts in their behalf. Responsibility, when properly felt, crushes not into silence and inactivity, but goads to effort.

Youth, impressible, ardent, earnest; full of glee and

gladness; just out from innocent childhood; swelling with ardor, ambition, and hopefulness; without experience, wisdom, or discretion; pressing toward manhood, eager to do its great work—who does not love it?

The world is soon to be theirs; who does not love to assist them to be in readiness for its duties? Where else can a word of wisdom and encouragement do so much good?

How beautiful is youth! Even the old remember it with joy, and recount its doings with grateful emotions, mingled a little with a feeling of uncensurable pride.

To me youth is full of rosy life and developing charms. I have scarcely passed its season of budding promise and flowing hope. All the impulses, hopes, anticipations, and aspirations peculiar to this ardent, sanguine, yet inexperienced age, are yet fresh in my mind. They are the memories of yesterday. They are mingled with the solemn duties of opening manhood. Hence the interests of youth are my interests; their feelings are my feelings; their good is my good. Our sympathies flow together; our objects in life are (or should be) the same. Our similarity of age forms between us a congeniality of spirit, thought, and action. This fact makes me feel that I may talk as a brother to my youthful friends, upon the realities of life which we are entering so nearly together. Will they not listen because I am one of them, if not for the wisdom of my words? If I have passed a little farther into the broad sea of life then my young friends, where the billows begin to roll and the breakers to rise, and am yet within speaking distance of them, and remember well the reefs I have passed, the shoals I have escaped, and the dangers I have seen, is it not my duty to send back over the waves my voice of warning and encouragement? Is it not my duty to speak in affectionate entreaty and counsel, as one fearfully conscious of the glories and dangers of the deep, deep sea of life, and solemnly impressed with the importance of every word he utters?

Life is a fixed fact, a stern and solemn reality. We are voyagers upon its broad, wild sea. Our bark is launched by other hands than ours. The currents of this great sea are all setting outward from the port we have left. The winds are off-shore, strong, and unchangeable. Go we must. We can neither stop nor turn back. The journey must be performed, whether we will or not. Resistance is as vain as it is impossible. It becomes us, then, to make the best of our voyage, to make it as profitable, pleasant, and delightful as we can. Regrets are idle; sighs are useless; murmurings are unwise. We can make it intensely delightful and almost infinitely profitable; or we can make it miserable, and a prodigal waste of the most precious means of enduring wealth. Wisdom's voice is for the most active diligence for both the profit and the pleasure of the voyage. She crieth against folly, sin, and a waste of precious time and energy. Minutes are diamonds. Strength is wealth. Opportunities are angel-visits of fortune. All should be seized upon with avidity, and turned to a good account.

The vessel we have set sail in is "fearfully and wonderfully made." Its architecture is divine. Its beauty is like a "fairy ship" of life, riding upon the waves of the "river of peace;" human words refuse to attempt its description. Its strength surpasses bars of iron and brass and bands of steel. Yet this ship may go down ere it reaches the haven beyond the sea. Its beauty may be marred; its strength wasted; its delicate workmanship defaced, ere the journey is half performed. Wisdom cries, beware! Her voice is for prudence, cleanliness, and temperance, and an active and watchful industry in beautifying and adorning the vessel; in making it airy, comfortable, and salubrious, in filling it with music and enriching it with the treasures of the pearl-caverned sea on which we glide, and for establishing the law of love for the control of all on board, that safety, happiness, and profit may be insured even till we turn our prow into the harbor of eternal peace.

The youth of to-day are the children of yesterday. The sports and frolics of yesterday have lost their relish this morning. They are too childish now. They have not meaning, importance, dignity enough. With the morning sun of youth there came a new order of feelings, a new class of desires, fresh, warm, impulsive, and clamorous. They ask for something they have not yet seen, or felt, or known. Our young friends look out into the world, and behold all is fresh, fair, and beautiful. They behold a field opening before them, wide and boundless as appears the vision of the future to the gaze of untaught eyes, and full of objects of interest that dazzle and bewilder the sight. They pant for the beauties and joys of this glorious, flower strown field of life. Which way they look they are delighted. Pleasure's hall, ambition's camp, love's rosy bower, mammon's mansion, learning's retreat, religion's sacred temple, all glitter on their sight; and the impulse within them is to go out and enjoy the realities that appear so entrancing to their view; as though to go out was to enjoy them.

Like a young mariner at the shore of the ocean, gazing out with a panting heart to be upon its mild, beautiful bosom, little dreaming that far in the distance it is nursing the storm and the whirlwind, to toss high his frail bark, and perhaps shatter it to atoms, is youth gazing forward upon the bright sea of life, which his young and untaught imagination paints before him. This is youth. It has great desires, but scanty means for giving them gratification; splendid visions of glory in the far-off distance, but little power to bring them within its reach; noble aspirations and glorious hopes, but little ability to attain their objects; mighty impulses for great and good achievements, but little wisdom and prudence to direct them; lofty conceptions of the attainments with which it would enrich its mind, the laurels with which it would crown its brow, and the honors with which it would mantle its shoulders, but little of that dauntless moral courage and firmness of purpose which are necessary to do battle with the ills and evils of time, and force a hard-earned victory out of the hands of life's relentless marauders. It is quick and impetuous, with little foresight; it sees every rose, but not the thorn; it is delighted with the beds of flowers about it, but knows not that the serpent is lurking below; it is in rapture with the rainbow, but dreams not that it is painted on a wreath of vapor; it has a wide-spread sail, but little ballast; a mighty force in the engine, but a pilot unused to the sea; it is rich in anticipated treasures, but poor in all that is requisite to obtain them; it is weak, while dreaming of strength; ignorant, while professing to much knowledge; pure, while unconscious that the miasmas of corruption are rising around it; innocent, confiding, and inexperienced, while not aware that smiling and deceitful tempters are lurking on every hand to lure it into the gilded walks of ruin and death. This being youth, and its beautiful but perilous situation, it appears but reasonable that every benevolent soul should endeavor to point out some of the dangers with which the young are surrounded, and suggest such courses of conduct, such principles of action, and inspirations to virtue and honor, as shall tend to render them safe, and direct their feet into the paths of peace, duty, and progress.

We are social beings, made to assist and encourage each other, as well as for mutual pleasure. If we each stood alone, apart from all others, like an isolated iceberg, and sought only our own happiness in a selfish, unamiable state of mind and course of conduct, how cheerless and forlorn would be our lives.

Little should we know of the real joys of soul, the solid bliss of life which we might possess by obedience to the dictates of our social nature. Advice, instruction, and encouragement are the best offerings of friendship to the young. And not the least of these is encouragement. With all its ambition and activity, youth is faint-hearted. It wants courage—calm, steady, moral courage—to go out in pursuit of its objects with a fearless confidence of success. Everywhere we find youth desiring good that it despairs of attaining. One's ambition is fired with the glory of a finished education, but he despairs of ever attaining his object, and so plods on in some ungenial calling, miserable and almost useless to society, without pursuing steadily and perseveringly his object. Another covets a profession, but despairs, and gives up from the same cause. Another would be a merchant, but has not courage to attempt what is the sole end of his ambition. Another would be a Christian in the high moral sense of that word, but the ideal of his holy ambition is so far above him that he despairs, forgetting that a daily progress, with such efforts as he might all the time put forth, would place him high among the ranks of the saintly followers of the Man of all goodness. Not one half of our youth are developing the full energy of their capacities; yea, nine-tenths are growing up in comparative undevelopment, not one half of their real capacity being called into action, from this one cause—a want of moral courage. They have energy, ambition, industry, but lack courage. An assurance from a valued friend, a word of cheer from a known and esteemed author, or a good-speed from the lips of experience, would be of essential service to them. It would fire their courage, and they would be true to their desires, their ambition, and duty.

I everywhere meet with faltering youth—noble souls, but fearful. Poverty, or diffidence, or the whims of unwise friends, or some fancied defect of mind or body, keeps them from the fields they desire to occupy, and where they could be more useful and successful than any where else in life, because their hearts are there. They lack true bravery of soul. Or, it may be in them, but it is undeveloped. Bravery, like all other virtues, is developed by the hand of culture. The noblest bravery in the world is moral bravery, that which meets disappointment, trial, affliction, failure, misfortune, sickness, and all the varied ills of life, with a determined and vigorous composure and a stern and trained self-reliance, which enable its possessor to pursue his even course undismayed, and add to, rather than detract from, his strength. Such a bravery is a lofty moral heroism, as great as that which nerved the martyrs' hearts and bared the reformers' stalwart arms. The bravery that faces the cannon's mouth is often the *fear* of public rebuke, or the love of public praise. Seldom is true bravery exhibited on the field of battle, or in any of the great conflicts of arms or minds carried on in the audience of the world. It is more generally ambition, fear of censure, love of gain, animal excitement, or the madness of narcotic or stimulating drugs or drinks. These supply the place of bravery, and the world knows not the difference. But there is a bravery that is true. It is the proudest, sublimest of human virtues. It is that bravery which dares be true to duty though the heavens come down; true when the world knows it not; true in the calm resolve of the midnight hour, when no eye but God's looks into the soul; true when the world would applaud for being false, and every worldly interest should seem to offer a price for cowardice. The bravery that under these circumstances is the same calm, undismayed, unseduced, dauntless vigor and determination of soul, is worthy the name, and is a godlike grandeur of moral greatness worthy a place in the calendar of the sublimest heroism. Our youth want more of this heroism. There is a fearful deficiency everywhere. It is as much needed in the common walks of life, as in the higher or highest pursuits, and often more so; for in public life the world often sustains the martyr, or the defender of humanity, or her injured rights; but in common life it is often that the severest trials have to be borne in solitary silence, while the contumely of neighbors, unjustly given, adds another trial scarcely less severe. To suppress the mutiny of the passions, to silence the clamors of lust, avarice, and ambition, to moderate the vehemence of desire, to check the repinings of sorrow, to disperse the gloom of disappointment, and suppress the dark spirits of despondency, requires a degree of vigorous moral courage that is not so often possessed as it is needed. It is everywhere needed, and very seldom possessed to a very great degree.

Whoever encourages this virtue in the world, either by example or precept, does the world good. The fear that its want inspires in nearly all youth, makes them often intensely miserable, subjects them to the doubt, and blackness, and torment of despondency, or "*the blues*," as they call it, and all the enervation, perversion of mind, waste of time, and ultimate evils that follow. Thousands on thousands of noble-minded and generous-hearted youth are ruined, or greatly injured by this prevailing cowardice. Scarcely any escape its scathing influence. Mere courage, determination, force of will, cheerful pursuit of known duties, or the objects of honorable desires, gladsome labor in the paths of right and usefulness, is the almost universal want among manhood, and especially among the young. Life is full of beauty, and ought to be of gladness. It has a thousand glorious joys, and as many sources of constant enjoyment. Constant cheerfulness is a duty. A faithful, joyful pursuit of the things that will minister most to our peace, usefulness, happiness, and progress, is a moral obligation that we ought to comply with all the time.

To encourage and enforce this duty, and strengthen its moral bearings upon the consciences of its youthful readers, is the chief object of this entire work. The youth of our country have no right to be unhappy; no business to be desponding; no sort of a privilege granted them by any constitution, either written or unwritten, in any of our States, or by any code of laws, natural or divine, to have "*the blues*," or to fail to pursue the objects of their honorable ambition. Our free institutions are designed to be the nurseries of youth, to afford them an open field and fair play for the legitimate and righteous exercise of their powers, in all the pursuits of high-minded industry. The friends of youth may, and will, encourage and advise them, through books, lectures, lessons, examples, and every known means of assistance; but depend upon it, young men and women, it is your own work, after all. Nobody else can do it for you. Fortunes are hewn out for ourselves, not made to order at a fortune shop. Characters are forged on the anvil of industry, by the well-directed strokes of the head and hand. Children are what they are made; but men and women are what they make themselves. The web of life is drawn into the loom for us; but we weave it ourselves. We throw our own shuttle and work our own treadles. The warp is given us; but the woof we make ourselves—find our own materials, and color and figure it to our own taste.

Every man is the architect of his own house, his own temple of fame. If he builds one great, honorable, and glorious, the merit and the bliss are his. If he rears a polluted, unsightly, vice-haunted den of devils, to himself the shame and misery belong. Success is the product of the sum of our years multiplied by our good actions. Life is a problem, and we solve it on the blackboard of the world. The answer we get at death, will approximate to the true one just in proportion to the correctness of our work. Every mistake, if not rectified, will carry us far from the truth. Errors in the commencement of the work are doubly dangerous, for by every succeeding step they carry us farther from the true end. Hence, we should start right in youth, that is, get a correct statement of the problem at which we must work while we live. We must not attribute our success to blind "*fortune*," or our failures to "*bad luck.*" Luck and fortune are mere words without any meaning. What is called "good fortune" is the result of sound judgment supported by a stout heart and a ready hand. "Bad luck" is the reverse of this.

Says an eloquent divine, in a lecture on Idleness: "I may here, as well as any where, impart the secret of what is called *good* and *bad luck.* There are men who, supposing Providence to have an implacable spite against them, bemoan in the poverty of a wretched old age the misfortunes of their lives. Luck forever ran *against* them and *for* others. One, with a good profession, lost his luck in the river, where he idled away his time a-fishing, when he should have been in the office. Another, with a good trade, perpetually burnt up his luck with his hot temper, which provoked all his employers to leave him. Another, with a lucrative business, lost his luck by amazing diligence at every thing but his own business. Another, who steadily followed his trade, as steadily followed his bottle. Another, who was honest and constant to his work, erred by perpetual misjudgments—he lacked discretion. Hundreds loose their luck by endorsing; by sanguine speculations; by trusting fraudulent men; and by dishonest gains. A man never has good luck who has a bad wife. I never knew an early-rising, hard-working, prudent man, careful of his earnings, and strictly honest, who complained of bad luck. A good character, good habits, and iron industry, are impregnable to the assaults of all the ill-luck that fools ever dreamed of. But when I see a tatterdemalion, creeping out of a grocery late in the forenoon, with his hands stuck in his pockets, the rim of his hat turned up, and the crown knocked in, I know he has had bad luck; for the want of all luck is to be a sluggard, a knave, or a tippler."

There is solid good sense in this extract, which ought to be learned by every youth. What countless thousands of old people are complaining of bad luck, in a peevish, sickly, disagreeable decline of life, which really is the legitimate result of the irregular, ill-directed, selfish, or vicious lives they have lived. Every youth should live with one eye on old age. If he should die before he gets there, it will never do him any injury. The moral principles of youth laid in store for age, will be just as valuable beyond death as this side.

Youth is a beautiful season of life. It is full of brightness, and radiant in smiles. It may well be compared to a mountain rill that has just left its bubbling source, which laughs and dances along amid the beauty and freshness of the upland scenery, kissing the flowers that dip their fragrant lips in its lucid waves, and smiling in the glad sunshine let in through the waving branches above it, before it reaches the great muddy stream to which it is unconsciously hastening.

This freshness and gladness that is so inherent in the youthful nature, should be carried into maturer life. What a charm it would add to middle life and old age, if it were so. Youth's outgushing gladsomeness, subdued by experience into a refined and happy tenderness, would be like flowers and fruits dallying amid the foliage of the same bough.

Whatever charms we now possess, we should retain

to adorn our characters through every succeeding stage of life. It is wrong to lay off the charms of youth in old age. Age should heighten every spiritual beauty; experience should subdue and soften it. Each year should add new adornments, but lay off none. Age should be more beautiful and happy than youth. And so it will be, if life is properly lived, if health is preserved, and the character every day beautified. A fretful, ignorant, unhappy old age is a proof of youthful errors and manhood blunders and views. It is the natural result of the life that has gone before it. If we live right, enjoyments increase with increasing virtue and wisdom.

Many of the springs of our purest happiness open in our affections. Every day should make these more pure, refined, and strong. The affections of youth are naturally volatile and liable to instability. In middle age, if they have been properly cultivated, they are deeper, warmer, truer, stronger, and enter into all the desires and plans of life; are the great substratum on which the solid masonry of life is built. In old age, they transfuse and transfix the whole being, shedding in all the chambers of the soul the soft, mellow light of a life's cultivation and refinement. This is what the God of love designed old age to be; that season of life in which the power and law of love should imbue and sway the whole soul; and if life is properly lived, this is what it will be. Affection, wisdom, and moral worth may all be augmented with the increase of years, and their triune glories so blended in age, that an angel beauty and blessedness shall be the crown to be worn into the company of cherubim and seraphim in the mansion of eternal progress and glory.

One thought here respecting the duties of youth to the world, as well as themselves. By an unalterable decree of nature, generations succeed each other upon the stage of action in quick and rapid succession. As the world is left by one, it is taken by the next. All its great concerns, however important and grand, are left to succeeding hands. The present generation is the product of the past. Into it is gathered the congregated wisdom of all that has gone before. Marked, peculiar, and brilliant are the accessions to the wealth of our time. Discoveries the most unexpected and wonderful, improvements the most useful and permanent, and advancements the most rapid, mark the developments of this age. Our fathers have astonished the world. In science, art, government, morals, religion, and every department of life, they have shown the proofs of their industry and principles. Noble and gratifying to the philanthropist and Christian are the evidences of the progress of our race in whatsoever is great and good. The present moment is pregnant with results greater than have yet been achieved. The wheel of progress has but just fairly started. It is rolling toward you, my young friends. Have you thought of it? It will soon be upon you. Have you ever thought that the world will soon be yours, with all its wealth and treasure, its pomp and splendor, its governments, laws, kingdoms, religions, philosophies, schools; its agriculture, commerce, arts, manufacturers, sciences, offices, honors, distinctions, principles? Have you thought that all, yes *all*, of that great, glittering, glorious thing which we call the world, will soon be yours, to use as you please—the legacy of the past bequeathed to your hands? If not, it is time you had thought of it. Your fathers and mothers will stay but little longer. Many of them are tottering now on the brink of the grave. A few days, and all will be yours. What will you do with it? Will you preserve its institutions of freedom, benevolence, learning, and religion? Will you cultivate well its fields and shops, and nurse its commerce, which now binds all nations together? Will you teach well its schools, inspire its youth with noble principles of piety and affection? Will you endow its colleges, fill its professorships, superintend its institutions of charity? Will you elect its officers of trust, administer justice, make laws, ordain decrees for nations? Will you establish boundaries, rear up states, form governments, and preserve the liberties of the people? Will you perform the sacred offices of religion, form churches, build sanctuaries, and fill the sacred desks with devout and pious men, who will administer the holy functions of their office in the fear of God and the love of men? Will you do all this, yea, all that is to be done in this wide world? You must do it, or it will not be done. There will be nobody else to do it. Are you preparing yourselves for this arduous, but glorious task? Are you cultivating your minds, endowing your hearts with great and good principles of action, principles of morality and religion? getting ready with stout, cheerful spirits for the work before you? Say, belle of folly and fashion, beau of the toilet and ball-room, reader of romance, visitor of saloons, lounger on couches, loiterer in shades, adorner of brothels, supporter of bars, scoffer of work, profaner of religion, despiser of law, breaker of the Sabbath, waster of time, and destroyer of body and soul; say, one and all of you, say, in the shining face of heaven, and in the presence of the great world which is descending into your hands, what are you doing to prepare yourselves for the discharge of the solemn and glorious moral duties before you? Stop in your thoughtless and sinful careers, and think a moment, just a moment. Will you help to keep the world in order, and urge it on apace in its sublime progress toward "the good time coming?" or will you hang like pestilential vampires to its heels, sucking out its moral life-blood and infusing poison in its stead, and retard, by the whole weight of your moral pollution and sin, its upward course?

My soul writhes in agony at what I see about me—youth in the lawless riot of demented folly, wasting time and strength, and mind and heart, in the pursuit of every thing but enduring good, as indifferent to the calls of true interest as duty, as lost to sober sense as shame, casting their idolatrous offering upon the profane altar of the good of this world. Oh, youth of glorious privileges, youth of free, noble America, rise up and stand for the true and the good! You have no time or strength to waste. Your duties are upon you. Evils are staring you in the face. It is yours to meet them with a noble defiance, and stay their progress of ruin. It is yours to abolish slavery, both mental and physical; to destroy intemperance; to revise our statutes; reform our penal code; make our prisons and penitentiaries asylums for the morally sick and insane; exterminate war, and all its concomitant evils, from the world; establish knowledge, religion, and free government in the uttermost parts of the earth; and bequeath to your children after you a legacy more rich and glorious than has descended upon you. Then your personal duties are not any less—yea, they are more; duties which involve the peace and happiness, and affect the very destiny of your souls, of those immortal, living, glorious essences, you call yourselves, and which came from the hand of the living and loving God.

This is a bird's-eye view of your duties. They are coming upon you. Their shadows fall before you; even now they are resting upon you. Though they are and bear the name of duties, they are the most delightful works to which young, moral intelligences can be called. Says a German philosopher, "The two most beautiful things in the universe are the starry heavens and the sentiment of *duty* in the human soul." As that sentiment is beautiful, so is the work to which it is called delightful. It is a work of sacrifice and effort, of labor and prayer; but it is rewarded with cheerfulness, joy, holiness, and an antepast of heaven.

LECTURE II.

MEDITATION.

The Seed-thought of Future Usefulness—True Mode of Meditation—Mental Impulses—Vacillation, the Ruin of Thousands—Pioneers of a New and Better Era—Propriety a Jewel—What Constitutes Virtue—The First Lesson of Youth—The Hopes and Glories of Youth—Noble, Self-poised Mentality—Power of Temptation—Self-denying Energy—A Truly Noble Character—A Pattern o Excellence.

I COME before you, my young friends, with a most reasonable thought, the first which should engage your attention, the thought out of which is to spring your after lives, the seed-thought of your coming usefulness. May I plant it? Will you lend me your ears to receive it, your minds in which to deposit it, your souls to sun it with attention, your hearts to water it with the dews of affection, that it may spring forth, bud, blossom, and bear the rich fruit of beautiful, glorious, happy lives? Here it is. Take it. It is, that life, young life, is commenced, truly, properly commenced, when the mind learns to *meditate*, to meditate upon what it is, upon what it would be, upon what it ought to be and may be. This is the starting-point of true life, mental life, spirit life; life directed by oneself, upward, onward, heavenward; life well-directed, soul-controlled, virtue-crowned, God-honored. To meditate is to think reasonably, reverentially, and calmly. To think is to commence to grow. To grow is to ascend toward heaven, to live as becomes a consistent, sentient, moral, and immortal being. To grow spiritually is the duty, work, and end of life. He who grows not is like a stunted tree in a barren soil, beautiless, flowerless, and fruitless. No green thing smiles around him, no refreshing spring opens within him. Such a life is not life. It is simple, barren being, scorched with sun heats, scathed with winds, and chilled with blasting colds, untutored, unblessed, unhonored, and uncheered with hope. To learn to be thoughtful, to *meditate*, then, is the first work of youth.

Meditation is here spoken of as opposed to all thoughtlessness, giddiness, impulsiveness; as opposed to all hasty, irreflective, careless habits of thought, feeling, and action. There is in youth in general an impulsiveness, a wild outbursting of native forces, all uncontrolled and free, which is highly detrimental to their best interests. And they are too apt to forget that these either may, or ought to be controlled. They are beautiful, grand, and glorious of themselves, even as the wild horse upon the prairie; but their usefulness depends upon their taming, upon the submissive docility and alacrity with which they yield to the honorable and fruitful labors of life. Thus harnessed to the noble car of utility and duty, they become majestic in their beauty and lovely in their gentle sublimity of power.

By the strong influences of these native, unborn forces

of the young soul, youth are too frequently driven from passion to passion, from habit to habit, evil to evil, and danger to danger, in rapid succession. To-day they are borne on the gale of the wildest pleasure; to-morrow, in hot displeasure, they foment discord and strife among each other, and nurse jealousies the most ungracious, and heart-burnings the most bitter and consuming. To-day they are more giddy than the feather tossed in the breeze, laughing as though they would burst at mere trifles, shouting and yelping like a herd of hounds, with as little restraint and about as little reflection, giggling, dancing, and grimacing, as though there were no such virtue as modesty, and decorum had become wholly obsolete; to-morrow, in darkness of spirit, despairing and wretched, because their thoughtless, hot-brained insanity of mirth has failed to give them peace and permanent joy, they wail over their luckless lot, and half curse their fate and stars and the day of their birth. To-day they plan some scene of merriment, some revel or riot, some bacchanal hilarity or epicurian gorge, some round of sport, or opportunity for giving vent to some darling passion, appetite, or habit, and indulge the imagination in all its lewd, wild revelings, about the objects of their thoughts; to-morrow they murmur because every thing went wrong, or are wholly occupied in attempting to conceal, or palliate something said or done, or are full of regrets about the mistakes and blunders of yesterday. They laugh or moan, dance or cry, sing or bewail, and give full vent and free rein to whatever impulse of feeling happens to be uppermost, changing more often than the wind, and reflecting as little upon their variations. Now the meditation that is counseled is the very opposite of all this, the antipode of this reckless, uncontrolled impulsiveness. This hot-brained haste has hurried on thousands of our most talented youth to wretchedness and utter ruin. Could they be called from the obscurity, depravity, and death into which they have been driven, they would come a long army of diamond souls, bedimmed and besotted in the dust and filth of earth. It would make angels weep to behold the array of ruin. The embryos of philanthropists, scholars, orators, statesmen, divines, rulers, kings and queens, would be seen in the solemn train. Dreary and sad the spectacle! To this host of sinburnt souls must daily additions be made, unless the youth of to-day learn to take rational heed to their steps, and meditate upon their ways.

The times call for high-born, self-controlled youth. The age beseeches for holy meditation, and calm resolution to its high duties, on the part of the rising generation. Nations are begging in solemn earnestness for nobler leaders. States are asking for wisdom and prudence to sit in their chairs of authority. The masses of mankind, bound by the chains forged in their own passion-fires, are crying for deliverance. Who shall answer these calls, but the youth of to-day? Who shall learn to control the world, and bear it upward, by first controlling themselves, and stepping, with eye bent above, upon the ladder of progress, but the youth of the nineteenth century? Never before were the calls upon the young so powerful and distinct to be the self-marshaled pioneers of a new and better era. The watch-word of that era must be self-government, instituted and established in the court of the soul by solemn meditation. Meditation should sit on the throne of the mind as the counselor of the mental powers; and thus, by early habits of obedience, even the passions will become powers of noble bearing and lofty mien, contributing an energy and determination that will wring victory out of every conflict, and success out of every struggle.

No reasonable objection can be made to the merriments, sports, and joys of youth; not even to its gleesomeness and out-leaping buoyancy of spirit. The objection lies against the *impulsiveness* of feeling with which these things are indulged in. The feelings come forth as wild masters, reckless and headstrong, and not as servants subdued, but strong and joyous. They should be submissive and obedient children of the *will*, yielding to its dictates, and doing its bidding with alacrity and power. Then the service they would render would be high and noble, the joy they would inspire rich and ecstatic. They would make the will more vigorous, the intellect more active, the affections more warm and deep, and the moral sense more vivid and strong. They should be made teachable and obedient, so they should be cool when commanded, resolute when called upon, ready to obey at all times the dictates of propriety.

Propriety is a jewel of the first water. Its graces are rich and rare. The youth who wears them is lovely and honored, and meditates well his ways. There is a time and place for every thing good; and in its time and place it is *good;* out of them, it is *evil.*

Merriment at a funeral, or in the hour of worship, is not only disgusting, but painfully abhorrent to all our kind and respectful feelings. There is a simple and beautiful *propriety,* pleasing to all, which gives grace to the manners, beauty to the person, sweetness to the disposisition, and loveliness to the whole being, which all should strive to possess. It is to be neither too gay nor too grave; too gleesome nor too sad; nor either of these at improper places. It is to be mirthful without being silly; joyous, without being foolish; sober, without being desponding; to speak plainly without giving offense; be grave without casting a shadow over others. In fine, it is to be just what every body loves and nobody dislikes, and just what makes us and others happy. This is propriety; and those who possess this richest flowering virtue of the soul, which breathes ambrosial sweetness along every walk of life, get the credit of possessing its counterpart, that rare quality of character honored everywhere, humbly christened "common sense," universally acknowledged to be the best of all sense.

Now, impulsiveness is absolute death to propriety, and a mortal enemy to common sense. It is always out of order, one side of the straight and narrow path, unpleasant to somebody, and unjust to some feeling.

To exhibit at all times the virtue of strict propriety, one must have every feeling in the most thorough and complete obedience to the purest rectitude and the most enlightened judgment. Our natural feelings are good; all our gushing sympathies, our tender sensibilities, are good and beautiful, and are the proper bases on which to build great and holy virtues. But they are not virtues of themselves, and we deserve no credit for their possession. They are gifts from the Parent Hand, and devoutly thankful should we be for their possession. The impulsive sympathy of the human heart is not a virtue. The spontaneous affections are not virtues. These are but the natural waters that flow freely from the springs within. To become virtues they must be chastened and trained to act, when and where and in such directions as enlightened judgment and moral sense shall determine. They must become the obedient children of the will, and be fixed on worthy objects. They must be refined and subdued to a sweet and all-pervading tenderness; refined by the meditative powers of the soul; refined by thought, by reflection, by effort, struggling by resistance of their impetuosity, by the soul's own resolute determination to master itself, and bring all its native forces into the service of virtue.

Sometimes to be still requires more virtue than to act. When the rich fruits, for which our desires clamor, hang temptingly on the boughs before us and within our reach, when all we have to do is to reach forth our hand and pluck and eat; when anger would rise in clamorous affray, ambition hold a lawless reign by unjust means; when avarice can bargain in fraud, and fill its coffers in an hour, then to say to these lawless waves, "Peace, be still," and be obeyed, requires oftentimes the most sublime resolves of virtue. Impetuosity usually overacts. But when all its spontaneities are subdued, as has been indicated, and made to conform to the dictates of enlightened judgment, we see that simple and beautiful propriety of action and deportment, which is so delightful everywhere, and which throws a spell of fresh and entrancing sweetness around its possessor.

This is the first lesson of youth, and hardest of all to learn, to subdue and chasten the inborn impulses of his soul. His soaring ambition, his reckless hope, his daring courage, his unbridled mirthfulness, all his impetuosities, he should early learn, should be held in check by the rein of sober sense. The curb and bit must be put on and drawn tightly. And this must be done by his own hand. In his hours of meditation he must form his plan, lay out his work, breathe his prayer for victory, and swear eternal fealty to his high purpose of right. In the still chambers of thought he must rally his moral forces, pledge them to duty, and call aid from above in his solemn work. It is his own work. No one else can do it for him. Others may assist him by encouragement, by advice, and solemn warning; but the work is his own. In the court of the soul it must be done. If he has learned this, and formed a resolution so to act, he is ready to start life's voyage with safety. He may launch out his boat, his rudder is hung, his compass is set, his sail is furled. If he has become a meditative being, a reflecting, reasoning, determining being, he has about him an element of safety, found nowhere but in himself. His wild impulses are bridled. He becomes calm, subdued, and dignified. The man, the true, the noble, Godlike man, begins to show itself in him. He has mastered himself, the most obdurate, willful, and reckless enemy he has in the wide world; or so nearly done it, that he has established the high council of law and right in his soul, to whose reign he has pledged an honorable fealty. He is ready to start a true life, to build a temple to virtue and honor, in which angels may delight to dwell.

Oh, how beautiful is the youth, who holds in check the impetuous forces within him, and makes them obedient to the calls of duty, propriety, and refinement! And, indeed, this is refinement! Even refinement, that charm of charms, which, worn about youth, makes it unspeakably interesting to all the world. To whom have poets dedicated their sweetest strains? To refined and virtuous youth. For whom hath music poured its most charming melodies? To noble youth. Whom hath art carved in marble, and painted in living light on the canvas? Beauteous youth. For whom are reared the halls of science? For aspiring youth. To whom does the states and kingdoms of the world look with anxious expectancy? To faithful youth. The world has thrown its great arms about its youth, and lovingly beseeches them to be wise and good, to reverently meditate upon the solemn realities in and about them.

To give a worthy response to this general and abiding

interest in youth, it is well that every one should have a living example of propriety and refinement before him; some one upon whom he can gaze continually, and receive constant supplies of noble influence. Who has not met with people whose every word is so well-timed, whose every action is so appropriate, whose every look beams with the evidences of such inward propriety, that they possess almost the power of captivation? Such we occasionally meet, and we meet them with open arms, and give them at once the confidence of old and long-tried friends. They should be our examples. We should impress their characters upon our own hearts. Now, this charm that dwells about such persons is the result of this self-directing, inward control, of which we are speaking. He who would be interesting to others, who would be truly great; who would possess a strong, noble, indwelling virtue, must control himself. And to do this he must meditate upon himself, study his own soul as he would a book, and determine all his internal forces according to enlightened judgment and rectitude. We ought to be capable of doing just as we wish to do. We ought to be so faithful to ourselves, so thoughtful, so ever guarded, so always ready, as to be able to determine our course of action, and control our deportment at will. What study of oneself, what thoughtfulness, what meditation upon the true excellencies of character, and what summoning of all the guards and forces of virtue within, are requisite to attain such control!

Let no youth think that this meditative effort is unnecessary in his case, because he is blessed with a well-balanced mental organization. An even, or equal balance among the mental powers, is often like the balance of a pair of scales. A feather's weight will determine it to one side. So in a mind of even development: a little influence will determine it to vice, and a little more to crime. Christ's was a perfect mind; it possessed a perfect balance among the mental powers; and yet he was tempted, strongly drawn by the forces of circumstances, and found it necessary to summon all his aids to virtue, and spend days and weeks in silent and lonely meditation and prayer. The wilderness saw his wrapt meditation, and the mountain heard his fervent prayer. Who else has communed with himself and his God with such intensity and constancy? Shall any of us then deem meditation unnecessary, because we have strong and well-balanced minds? "Let him that thinketh he standeth, take heed lest he fall." Let none give heed to that awful, damnable, moral heresy, that *outward circumstances must be all-controlling*. If it were so, then we could never have had a Christ. If it were so, then Washington would never have resigned the throne of absolute dominion in a nation's heart. If it were so, the world never would have known the benevolent Howard. It was resistance of outward circumstances that made these men and made Christ. It is resistance of evil influence that makes virtue. America owes its freedom and its civil and religious blessings to a resistance of evil circumstances. Say not that there is no power in the human soul to resist both outward and inward evil. It is moral heresy, rank and black. Man can meditate upon his ways, and by forethought and resistance beat down the barriers to virtue that rise in his path, and be what he ought to be, a student and master of himself and the world. Phrenology declares this. The Bible declares this. Universal human experience declares this; and reason knows it. When this is attained, the highest order of virtue is reached, a great moral force is acquired, without which there can be neither great virtue nor perfection of character. Says the great and good Dr. Channing on this subject: "It is worthy of especial remark, that without this moral energy, resisting passion and impulse, our tenderest attachments degenerate more or less into weaknesses and immoralities; sometimes prompting us to sympathize with those whom we love in their errors, prejudices, and evil passions; sometimes inciting us to heap upon them injurious praises and indulgences; sometimes urging us to wrong or neglect others, that we may the more enjoy or serve our favorites; and sometimes poisoning our breasts with jealousy or envy, because our affection is not returned with equal warmth. The principle of love, whether exercised toward our relatives or our country, whether manifested in courtesy or compassion, can only become virtue, can only acquire purity, consistency, serenity, dignity, when imbued, swayed, cherished, enlarged by the power of a virtuous will, by a self-denying energy. It is inward force, power over ourselves, which is the beginning and end of virtue."

This is the power and dominion we should strive to obtain. It should be the great object of every youth. It is a work of great moral grandeur; and is the result of the most dignified and sublime action of the will, of judgment directing the course, and conscience resolutely declaring that it must be complied with. It is this self-control by the moral energies of the understanding which is counseled as the object of meditation. And more stress is laid upon it, because here lies the chief beauty of every action, the rarest excellency to be attained by the human soul. Whatever in human character is worthy of confidence, to which we bow with deep and holy respect, is to be attributed to the presence of this inward moral force.

When we see a youth purely and truly honest, amid strong temptations; calm and composed amid the stormy elements of passion; serene and pure amid the incitements to lustful desire; unmoved and courageous amid alarming dangers; resigned and trusting in the hour of sorrow; patient under severe trials and burdens; self-possessed at all times, saying to passion, to appetite, to all the impulses of his young and ardent nature, "Peace, be still!" and resolutely forcing them to obey, we see a sight more truly noble than any warrior or conqueror the world ever nursed on her bloody bosom, and one that in the eye of God is greater than any king or emperor that ever sat upon the throne of ambition's dominion.

Who will strive for this inward control, this mastery of self, this enthronement of conscience over all the impulses of our nature? Let him meditate long, well, and deeply, upon what he is, and what he ought to be; upon virtue, duty, life, and destiny. Let him early learn to hold council within himself over every desire and impulse that rises within him, over every action of the soul, and see that at all times obedience is yielded to the dictations of this council. To be successful in this, he must be always watchful, always guarded, always striving for the more perfect attainment of the great object before him. At home and abroad, in the field and in the shop, in the hour of pleasure and the season of sorrow, in prosperity's day and adversity's night. in confidential intercourse with companions and friends, and in the treatment of enemies and defamers, he should enthrone his will, and put forth every power within him, to be just what he should be. Has he a pattern of excellence before him, some friend, some acquaintance, some illustrious character, whom he would imitate? Then let that character be perpetually before him, like a Divine Omnipresence. Let him remember the perfect pattern, the "Man Christ Jesus," "the One altogether lovely, the chiefest among ten thousand," and strive always to conform to that pattern. It is within the power of nearly every youth to be great and good, to be pure and excellent, to moderate the vehemence of every desire, chasten every feeling, subdue every passion, restrain every impulse, and curb every wayward tendency. All that is necessary to accomplish this, is firmly to determine upon the object, and persevere in carrying it out.

ECTURE III

THE DANGERS OF IMPULSE.

The Dangers of Impulse—Obstacles to Virtue—Evils of Ungoverned Passions—Criminality the Fruit of Impulse—Restraint of the Animal Passions—Enthronement of Morality and Intelligence—Self-government the Soul of Progress—Public Evil flows from Individual Vice—Our Future in the Hands of our Youth.

On the outposts of the human soul, its great Author has wisely stationed a sentinel, whose duty it is to watch for *danger*. When faithful, it warns of both physical and moral danger. Its eye is as an eagle's, and its heart sensitive, and easily alarmed. But, strange as it may seem, many youth have deemed it cowardly to listen to the warnings of this noble watchman of the mental family, and have turned a deaf ear, till the watchman has ceased his cry, and the sacred soul-sanctuary has been overrun by enemies from without and within.

Youthful reader, are you one of this unwise number? Does the cry of this sentinel ring through the arches of your soul, warning of the danger of impulse, and rehearsing in your ears the miserable results of its impetuosities? If not, call him to duty; for above all things else, you need his friendly admonitions.

The dangers of impulsiveness are not chimerical. They are real, positive, and awful. Who does not know that the devil has pitched his camp within us, and made our impulses his imps of ruin? What else but impulse led our Eden mother from the bower of innocence and virtue? Where else but on the tree of impulse grew the fruit she ate, which turned to ashes on her lips? What else was the "knowledge of evil" she acquired but the results of impulse; and what else was the "knowledge of good" thus obtained but the blessings of self-control? Has her sad experience given us no warning? Has the recklessness of the whole world given us no alarm? It is time to take warning. This age is pregnant with some great good. What is it? It travails for delivery. Feel we not already, therefore, inspiration of its embryo good? Is it not a deliverer for youth, a divine lawgiver for the young soul, to re-establish in it the Eden-trampled throne of self-dominion, to crown thereon imperial Right and Duty as king and queen, who shall bridle the impulses for the soul's everlasting servants? Let the warnings of the past, and the developments of the present, bid us hope for so great a good.

Little are many youth aware of the obstacles to the approach of this "good time coming," the obstacles which they permit to exist within themselves. There are thousands of youth of good motives, generous desires, honorable ambition, who hate meanness, despise a vicious course of life, who are yet in very great danger from their impulses. A temptation a little stronger than they have met, an evil a little more seductive, a moment a little more unguarded, may work their ruin; or if not work absolute ruin, may plant thorns of moral poison that will sting them with a thousand regrets, and cause the blush to mantle the faces of all their best friends.

All very impulsive persons live perpetually among thorns. They do and say things almost daily that cause themselves, or somebody else, most sore disquietude. When they are so stupid as not to see the improprieties of their own course, they may be causing frequent and deep wounds in the hearts of all who love them best. How often an impulsive person wounds the feelings of his truest friends! His thoughtless words, poisoned, it may be, with the gall-drops of a fit of anger or jealousy, envy or pride, or a momentary flash of displeasure, may cut like two-edged swords to the heart's core. Or, wanting that sweet refinement given by self-control, their very roughness and harshness may "grate horrible discord" in the ears of those that love him, and would gladly be charmed by his sweet words of wisdom and goodness.

How much, oh, how much unhappiness is thus caused by the uncontrolled waywardness of impulsive natures! If we were to probe the hearts of all refined and sensitive natures, and express what we should find, we should reveal a great world of misery that is all unexposed to human gaze now. In the secret, silent chambers of the purest, loveliest souls, these sorrows are felt, and felt with a keenness all unknown to less refined and sensitive minds. And what is worse, we thus cause our loveliest and most truly excellent friends to suffer. How mortifying is the thought that such friends are pierced with anguish, occasioned by our want of self-control, by the reckless impulses we nurse within us. Go into the homes of men, where the world's eye is shut out, and see the desecration of love's hallowed sanctuaries; see companions estranged; see brothers and sisters living as strangers to each other, performing none of those little offices of love that are so sweet and delectable; see children growing up in an atmosphere of icy coldness, and learn the evils of ungoverned passions. Go again into the world, and witness the strifes, animosities, quarrels, and disgusting scenes of neighborhood disturbances, and another similar lesson may be learned. Friendships are broken, which long years of faithful confidence and good offices had cemented; and affections are estranged, which a thousand cords of tenderness had bound. There is hardly a danger to which youth is exposed, to which the great avenue does not open from the fruitful source of some passion-fire. Read the history of criminals, of all the most unfortunate classes of beings, and you will find that impulse was the rock on which they split. Their first digressions from rectitude were not premeditated. They were the works of haste, of thoughtless impetuosity. They were often yielded to as innocent, were even regarded as sprightly, as evidences of wit, or genius, or strong affection, and not unfrequently have been imitated by admiring companions. There is a wild, untamed beauty about these impulsive feelings, that often causes youth to admire and imitate them. And they frequently have much the appearance of virtue in their exhibitions, when they are fast leading those who are nursing them on to ruin. Look at the thousand sorrowful cases of intemperance, spread like wrecks on the ocean's bottom, all over the length and breadth of our land; look at the thousand victims of lust of both sexes still more disgusting and degraded; at the unfortunate victims of criminal desire and unhallowed passion for confirmation of what has been said. Yea, look at the late most deplorable case of Professor Webster, over which a nation has mourned, and which has blasted the hopes and happiness of a refined and beautiful family, and believe there is danger in impulse. The early impulsiveness of the late Henry Clay, a genius of lofty powers and commanding brilliancy, kept him from the presidential chair, and from almost unexampled admiration and glory. Living statesmen might be mentioned of equal power and eminence, whose glory is tarnished, and whose throne in the nation's heart is feeble and tottering, from the same cause. Oh, that youth could understand these things! Many of them are encouraging the most ruthless marauders in their own breasts. Almost every circle of youth exhibits examples of unbridled impulses. A want of reflection, of thought, of moral force, is visible almost everywhere.

This argues that vice, crime, and wretchedness are to fill up the next page of human history. We talk of reformation, of progress; but little can be our advancement, till youth are taught a strong and vigorous resistance of the rude dominance of the passions. Here is the very place to begin. First of all come the appetites, the general feeders of animal desire. These are pampered in a thousand ways and forms from earliest childhood. Thev foster a pervading animalism. They stimulate the propensities. They feed the fires of passion. The influence of pampered appetite is a viewless miasma of disease, bringing the entire mind under its death torpor. To make a character what it should be, the moral and intellectual nature should be enthroned. The man should rule the animal. To establish and preserve such a government within us, is the noblest work of human attainment. To resist strong impulses, to subdue powerful passions, to silence the voice of vehement desire, is a strong and noble virtue. And the virtue rises in height, beauty, and grandeur, in proportion to the strength of the impulses subdued.

True virtue is not always visible to the gaze of the world. It is often still and calm, like the rolling tide of a mighty river. "There are seasons," says the great author already quoted, "when to be still, demands immeasurably higher strength than to act. Composure is often the highest result of power. Think you it demands no power to calm the stormy elements of passion, to moderate the vehemence of desire, to throw off the load of dejection, to suppress every repining thought when the dearest hopes are withered, and to turn the wounded spirit from dangerous reveries and wasting grief, to the quiet discharge of ordinary duties? Is there no power put forth when a man, stripped of his property, of the fruits of a life's labor, quells discontent and gloomy forebodings, and serenely and patiently returns to the tasks which Providence assigns? I doubt not that the all-seeing eye of God sometimes discerns the sublimest human energy under a form and countenance which, by their composure and tranquillity, indicate to the human spectator only passive virtues." Individuals who have attained such power, however they may be viewed among men, are among the great ones of God's children. They are the Washingtons of humanity.

One of the prominent missions of this age seems to be to develop the *individual man*. The individual in times past has been lost in the mass. Now he is beginning to be recognized. A single man in the eye of God is as important as a race. Man is a microcosm. He has a world in himself. He is an epitome universe. To develop a race, each individual must be developed. The development of the individual effects the development of the race. So the government of the individual effects the government of the race. Government is at the bottom of progress. The state or nation that has the best government progresses most. So the individual who governs best himself makes the most rapid progress. Progress is a necessary result of true government. The native energies of the human soul press it to activity. Activity is its primal law. When these energies are controlled, they rush onward in the path of progress with the celerity of thought. Nothing prevents their movement. Like the calm rolling river, they press onward, filling full the channel in which they are destined to move. No counter-currents of passion and back-eddies of disorderly impulse keep them back. No juttings in of bluffs, no settings back of coves, caused by the first storms of impulse, prevent their steady career.

Government is but another name for harmony; and harmony but another name for heaven. Mental harmony is the goal of human perfectibility. It is the balance of all the mental powers in subjection to the will. It is the result of the self-control we are so earnestly recommending. Individual harmony is necessary to effect the social harmony of the masses. We complain of the antagonisms of society, the distrust, animosity, and degredation, all through the social compact. This is wrong; the fault is with the individual. The inharmony is in the single soul. Make the individual harmonious and you make the community harmonious. Is the water of the river bitter? It is so because the springs from the mountains send forth bitter streams. Chide not the river till the springs are sweetened.

Does society need reorganizing? Is its present organization base and antagonistic? It is because antagonisms exist in the individual. Organize society upon a closer basis; it will be but bringing firebrand in closer proximity with firebrand, and raising higher the flame of discord. Society is wrong in its organization, fundamentally wrong. But it is so because of the wrong in its individuals. Our social organization is on a level with the individuals composing it. Organize a true government in each individual soul; make harmony there and social harmony will follow, and follow just in proportion to individual progress.

Where shall we begin in the great reformation, except with the youth? Society is daily passing into their hands,

Its great concerns will soon all be theirs. To reform it they must reform themselves. To reform themselves they must control themselves. Reform means control. The drunkard reforms when he controls his appetite; the libertine, when he controls his lust; the thief, when he masters his covetous desire. The great work of human reform, in all its length and breadth, its height and depth, its magnitude and importance, is comprehended in the self-control here recommended to youth. Oh, youth of America! See you the vast importance of this enthronement of reason and conscience, this establishment of law and order within the realms where you are the rightful rulers? See you that your own prosperity, peace, and happiness, that the harmony and progress of the social compact, and the usefulness, power, and glory of your country, are to be measured by the degree of wisdom and moral force with which you control and direct the mighty and immortal powers which God has placed in your hands? Be entreated to perpetual vigilance in your own behalf. Be pointed to the aids about you for assistance in this work; to the experience of the world, the wisdom of age, the instructions of science, the great examples of virtue, the Word of God, the name and character of Christ, the teachings and spirit of His gospel, the still sanctuaries of the soul in its calm moods of thought. All bid you meditate upon your ways, and be wise and virtuous, that you may grow into temples of spiritual beauty and everlasting peace.

LECTURE IV.

FORMATION OF CHARACTER.

Life is for a Purpose—A useless Life—What is Character?—Character Self-made—Duty of Parents—Chance Character always Evil—Choice of Vice or Virtue open to all—Will or Circumstance Clothe the Mind—Goodness the only Source of Happiness—Character is "catching"—Inter-relation of Minds—Power of silent Influence—Way to do Good to the World—Molding Immortal Minds—Every One can be a Benefactor—All intended to be Happy—A vicious Course one of Difficulty—Vice respects Virtue—Character the Soul's Habiliment—Character Eternal.

It is well to pause on the threshold of life, and ask ourselves *why we live.* Life means something. It is charged with eternal significance. It is big with sublime realities. Every step is a word, every day is a sentence, every week is an oration, every year is a book, full of meaning as the sun is of light. Life is a book; and we write in it something, be it much or little, sense or nonsense. And what we write we can not unwrite. Our pen is time—our ink is indelible. What we write we write, and do it for eternity. Life is not mean—it is grand. If it is mean to any, he makes it so. God made it glorious. Its channel He paved with diamonds. Its banks He fringed with flowers. He overarched it with stars. Around it He spread the glory of the physical universe—suns, moons, worlds, constellations, systems—all that is magnificent in motion, sublime in magnitude, and grand in order and obedience. God would not have attended life with this broad march of grandeur, if it did not mean something. He would not have descended to the blade of grass, the dew-drop, and the dust-atom, if every moment of life were not a letter to spell out some word that should bear the burden of a thought. How much life means, words refuse to tell, because they can not. Youth have stepped upon its threshold. Ought they not to ask, why they live—for what object? The very doorway of life is hung around with flowery emblems, to indicate that it is for some purpose. The mystery of our being, the necessity of action, the relation of cause to effect, the dependence of one thing upon another, the mutual influence and affinity of all things, assure us that life is for a purpose to which every outward thing doth point. But do men study the meaning of life? Do they find out for what they live? Some there are, scores of them, who appear to live as brutes live, for naught but because life is in them, and remains there. They have an instinctive disposition to live, and so they do live. But for what, they know not, nor seem to care. They neither ask what they are nor what they ought to be. They take no solemn thought of to-day, nor forethought of to-morrow. They live for what? Ask them. For nothing. Their lives are the sport of what is around them. See that thistle-down dancing on the breeze, hither, thither, up, down. It is an emblem of their lives. They aim at nothing. They live for no purpose. They move by no unvarying principle. They carry out no plan of life. They have no plan. Life to them is a mazy web-work of circumstances. They fix no mark at which to strike. They run, and gain no race. They work, and accomplish nothing. They speak, but who regards it? They make much noise and bustle, but who care for them, more than to get out of their way? They have friends, but they are worth nothing. They live among neighbors, but they are nuisances. If they stay at home, nothing is done; if they go abroad, nobody values them. They walk about among men as other people, but they leave no track behind them. Their judgment is not respected, their friendship is not wanted, their hatred is not feared. Nobody cares for them but the politician at the election, and the sexton at their burial. What are they? To themselves, nothing; to the world, nothing. And yet they work as hard as any body, talk, and feel as much as their neighbors, and have a great deal more trouble. Many such there are; and they seem to be just what they are, because they live for nothing. They have not learned the meaning of life. They have nothing in particular to be or do, and hence are and do nothing in particular. They have no character to form or sustain, no profession to fill, no trade to follow. Many of them are industrious, well-meaning people, of fair abilities and respectable feelings. But they lack the one thing needful, an object in life, something to live for.

No youth who has learned the meaning of life is ambitious to fill the place of such people. Are you, my reader?

But let us ask, *what is the purpose of life?* We answer, *it is the formation of a genuine character.* By this we mean a real inbred cast of soul, not a *reputation;* for one may have a reputation for that which he is not.

The knave may be reputed an honest man. The villain may be believed to be good. The hypocrite may have a reputation for what he appears to be. The fop, the dandy of the tailor, may pass for a veritable man.

Character is what a man is; reputation is what he is thought to be. Character is within; reputation is without. Character is always real; reputation may be false. Character is substantial and enduring; reputation may be vapory and fleeting. Character is at home; reputation is abroad. Character is in a man's own soul; reputation is in the minds of others. Character is the solid food of life; reputation is the dessert. Character is what gives a man value in his own eyes; reputation is what he is valued at in the eyes of others. Character is his real worth; reputation is his market-price.

If the attainment of reputation was the true object of life, it might be one magnificent game of deception and hypocrisy. Men would smile in villainy, and pray with the hand on the dagger's hilt. He who lives for fame is as likely to be a devil as a man, and far more so. He is a beggar, asking that which he ought to possess at the hands of others. He lives for the shadow, and not the reality. Fame that is lived for is a bubble, hollow and thin, which bursts in attempting to secure it. To live for fame is to miss it. To make this the object of life is to fail. Real fame, that is substantial, is that which follows, not that which is run after; that which comes, not that which is sought. He who lives for fame lives in vain, for he ends life poor as he commenced it, and often poorer, for he has robbed himself of innocence, and clothed his soul in the red garments of guilt. He has sacrificed his soul's health for the disease of sin.

No, not for this should man live, but for real character, for worth of soul, for wealth of heart, for the diamond-dust of mind. He should live to be what be ought to be, and do what he ought to do; live to make his soul great and good, to clothe it in the garments of light, and fill it with the warmth of love. Then fame will come delighted to crown him with her wreaths of honor. Then reputation will shake hands with character, and the twain will be one forever.

A man's character is what he makes for himself; it is his own workmanship; it is the statue of the man of his conception, which he carves in the studio within. It is the man he paints on the soul's canvas. God makes the soul; man makes the character. The child-soul is without character. It is a rudimental mental existence, pure as the driven snow, beautiful as a cherub angel, spotless, guileless, and innocent. It is the chart of a man, yet to be filled up with the elements of a character. Those elements are first marked on it by its parents or guardians. They limb out the first rude sketch of a character. With what delicacy should they use the pencil of parental influence, in sketching the outlines of their child's character! The young soul is soft, and the lines they make are deep, and not easily erased. It is a man they form. Responsible work! It is an immortal soul they work upon, destined to survive the wreck of matter and the crush of worlds, and bear on its face, forever, at least some distant traces of their work. Solemn thoughts! Parents, what are you doing? Making folly-marks on thy child's soul? Scribbling for sport? Blackening it with passion? Staining it with error? Indifferently casting it out among the circumstances of a crazy world, to be marred and defaced by such marks as they may make upon it? Pause in thy work for sober reflection. Open thy soul in prayer for Divine help; for it is on the canvas of God's make that thou art making thy marks. Form for your child the outlines of a character that, if exposed in the sunlight of the celestial world, where it will surely appear, you will not be ashamed of.

When a child becomes a youth, it assumes the formation of its own character. It puts in its hand to paint with the parents. And gradually it crowds away the parental hand, when it takes the whole responsibility itself, and becomes its own master. Now the youth works for himself. He has become his own man. His character is in his own hands. He molds it as he will. If he does it well, the joy and the glory are his. If he does it ill, the sorrow and the shame are his. He can not shuffle off the responsibility. Neither earth nor heaven holds a being upon whom he can load it. God made his soul, his parents formed for him the outline of a character, and now it is for him to fill it up, and finish it, as best he may; to make it a dark picture of vice and woe, breathing the malaria of guilt and shame, or to brighten it with a living beauty and glory that shall make it an ornament for the parlor of heaven. Yes, it is his work. Doubt it not, O youth.

He must make his own character, build himself, rear the fabric of that building, in which he shall dwell, and which shall be known as his spiritual home. Some say that circumstances make character. I grant they do in many instances. But who that is wise will trust them? Circumstances are blind, brainless, and irresponsible. They are more likely to make a bad than a good character, for they confer no self-respect nor self-control, without which any character is miserably deficient. Characters formed by circumstances are much like machine poetry. They will do for the sport of mirth, and the torment of the sense of the beautiful. But they are horrible things. It makes angels weep to look at them. They are the picture of old chaos, a mass of confusion. A thousand winds have blown together the materials of which they are made. They usually lack order, harmony, consistency, and beauty, the very elements and essentials of a good character. We had a picture of them at the commencement of this discourse—those aimless nuisances that live for nothing, and mold, and become putrid, about the sewers of the world. If ought on earth is despicable, it is these porous masses of conglomerated filth and scum that float on the surface of society, driven or attracted by every speck of circumstance about them. They are purposeless, powerless, enervated automatons, playing second fiddle to chance. One brave will to resist evil and hold fast to good, is worth a million of them. One stout soul, with a resolute determination to make its own character, after the pattern of its own high-wrought ideal, that, Jackson-like, takes the responsibility of being what suits its well-formed judgment, is of more real significance than an army of them. It will stand against them, and defy their power.

Heed not a moment the sophistical advocate of the omnipotence of circumstances. It is an atheistical sophism, as dishonorable to man as to God. It robs both of power, and the universe of an intelligent will. It makes men puppets, dancing to the discordant jargon of circumstances, and God the auditor, looking on well pleased with our fantastic capers, which are made because we can not help them, as the wires are pulled by the presiding circumstances. One moment's sober reflection will tell you that you can set your foot on circumstance, and preside over yourself. You can say to the tempter, "Begone," and compel him to depart. You can study the stars, or plow the earth; read the moral lessons of Jesus, or the language of lust from a wanton's face; go to the school or the tippling-shop; listen to Socrates or Epicurus, as you please. You can will to take the upper or the lower road, the path of virtue or of vice.

Circumstances do control countless thousands, but it is not necessarily so. They yield because they do not try to oppose. They wage no war with evil. They cast no missiles against them from a resolute will. It is true, a youth may be what he pleases. He may be good or evil, be wise or foolish, intelligent or ignorant. He may make himself a good or a bad character. He may beautify or deface his soul. It is for him to do as he will. Youth are their own choosers of character. There are good and bad, high and low, virtuous and vicious. The youth is left to his own choice; or he can close his eyes, fold his arms, and let chance clothe his soul with a character. The new-born soul is naked. Character is the garment it puts on. It must be clothed; if it clothes not itself, others will clothe it. There are two ways to obtain the clothing—will and circumstance. Which will you choose, O youth? You can choose a good character, or you can choose a bad one, or you can trust to circumstance, and run the risk. It is an awfully hazardous risk, and almost sure to lose, or fail. Settle it at once, my young reader, which you will choose; settle it early, in wisdom and prayer. The choice is one of priceless moment. If a globe of gold, as large as our earth, and one of dross, were before you, for you to choose which you would have, the choice would not be one millionth part so important as the choice of a character. What are gold, gems, crowns, scepters, and honors, put on with human hands, compared with the character with which the soul is clothed. These are well enough, and administer to human happiness or misery according to the circumstances of their possession. But they are not necessary. They are trifles that please human children, as toys do babies. But they vanish with the using. They are like the boys' fire-crackers, which explode with the noise that delights. But not so with character. It is the *essential* of happiness. Without a good character happiness is never known. All that exalts, ennobles, embellishes, and dignifies humanity—all that confers solid peace, real joy, soul-felt satisfaction—all that good men and angels love and admire in human creatures, is blended in the beauty and glory of a truly good and genuine character. Whatever degree of happiness of "the soul's calm sunshine and heart-felt joy" is felt by any man, is the result of a corresponding degree of goodness in his character. Good men may have their trials and sorrows as well as others; but in and through them all there is the sunshine of a holy and lofty peace above all clouds, as permanent and glorious as the firmament of heaven. Their troubles are the earthly incidents of strong affections and noble aspirations, which refine and elevate while they cause pain, so that in the end they increase rather than diminish their real happiness.

There is no happiness except that which results from goodness—intellectual, moral, and affectionate goodness—or, in other words, from the true, the good, and the affectionate in character. All the treasures of ten thousand worlds like this will not compare in value with one good character—with one pure heart, for the production of all that is satisfying and blessed. They will not purchase peace, nor joy, nor sacred rest, nor the sweet tranquillity of an unsullied conscience, nor one single moment's real bliss. They can never be exchanged for those golden-gloried virtues that blossom all over a good character, like the blossoms on a thick bed of roses, and which are as rich in the sweet incense that the heart loves most, as the flowers are in refreshing fragrance. No, naught can stand up to be compared with a good character, either for intrin sic beauty, imperishable value, or the production of the fruits of solid and enduring serenity and joy of soul.

The youth who places a proper estimate upon a good character, has learned a lesson that is more valuable to him than any thing else possibly can be. He has learned the source of his purest joys.

But the happiness and blessedness of a good character are not confined to the sunny chambers of its possessor. Character is catching. If one has a good character, he gives something of its goodness to all with whom he associates. If his heart is radiant with the light of virtue, that light gets out, and shines in upon the hearts of others. He can scarcely look at another without impressing some mark of his own character on the heart of the one upon whom he gazes. A man's face is almost always radiant with the light of his true character. Character, like murder, will out. It can not long be concealed. You might as well attempt to chain the lightnings in the black caverns of the surcharged cloud, or put a hood over the great bright face of the sun, as to lock up a man's character from the sight of his fellows. God never designed that it should be. Character was made to be seen. It is the government of the soul, put on, not only for the comfort and convenience of the wearer, but for the pleasure of other people's eyes. It is not worn for self alone, for that would be mean, but for all by whom it is surrounded. The human soul can not be seen, nor do I believe it ever will be by human eyes, not even in heaven, but only its garments, which are its character. They show, and will show the real state of the soul, its form, its power, its purity, love, and mental nature. The character will always be visible—here, partially, in the spirit world, completely. Even now the character shines through the gross material of the flesh. "The human face divine" is like the dial-plate of a clock; it tells the state and position of the machinery behind. It publishes to the world the character of the dweller within. It is in vain for any man to think that he hides his character. He may for a few days deceive others with respect to its nature; but the unseen influence which he exerts upon those about him is exactly in keeping with his real character. There is an invisible telegraph between soul and soul—a mysterious spirit-medium by which the secret states of our mind are unconsciously conveyed to another to produce there their legitimate influence. Sometimes this secret influence is so powerful that we feel it sensibly, and yet know not why. How often, when we have met a stranger, have we been impressed with feelings, the cause of which we could not explain. Sometimes it is a charm, sometimes a feeling of repulsion. There can be no doubt but it was the spiritual influence of that stranger's character, darted into our spirits along the invisible wires that God has laid between the souls of His children. It is by this unseen and mysterious process that the mightiest influences of characters are exerted about us. Sometimes we call this influence sympathy, sometimes love, sometimes repulsion, sometimes pleasure, sometimes pain. But when we give it these names, it is felt in its strongest power. When we name it not, when we feel it not, and know it not, it is at work. It is always on its sleepless mission. Then how solemn the thought that our characters are all the time operating upon all with whom we associate, whether we will or not.

It is not necessary that we shall be public speakers, or writers, or functionaries, in order that our influence shall be felt about us. These outward means of influence are more direct and apparent, but not more positive and sure. Our looks, our words, our actions, even our silence, speak of our characters. We are impressing ourselves upon others. Our seniors, our equals in age and standing, and even the little children about us, are receiving impressions of our characters. We are breathing a silent but strong influence into many a soul, which goes direct from our characters. Are not our responsibilities fearful, so great and constant is our influence? And hence the vast, the inexpressibly vast, importance of possessing good characters. Our characters are not for ourselves only, but for others. If they make us happy, they produce a similar happiness in the minds of all with whom we associate, differing only in degree. Think of our friends, relatives, and neighbors about us, the dear little children, the circles in social and business life we enter daily, weekly, yearly; think how many we meet with, speak with, and thus influence, from year to year, all through our lives, and then calculate the amount of influence we exert upon the world. And then think that through all whom we have thus affected, our influence, in a smaller degree, is carried to all whom they do or may influence, and thus outward and onward, till it may be that generation from generation, even through eternal ages, shall feel the wave of influence which we have set in motion, and then endeavor to realize the responsibility that rests upon us. If our character is bad, oh, what a weight of wickedness and misery we shall cause; but if good, how pleasing the thought that we are thus instrumental in sending tide after tide of joy and peace out on the wings of our virtuous influence, to purify and gladden human hearts in countless thousands, and for as many ages. No thought to me is more rife with a solemn grandeur of interest, than that which relates to the influence I am silently exerting upon my fellow-creatures. And none so burdens my soul with the conviction of my moral responsibilities as this. Would that my readers could properly appreciate it. The object of this lecture is to duly impress the importance of a strongly and positively good character. Not only does our self-love dictate this importance, but every feeling of philanthropy and humanity in our hearts, and every aspiration which we possess, and every hope that glows within us, for the progress and happiness of our race, presses home with solemn earnestness its fearful and glorious greatness.

Would we do good to the world? Then let our characters be formed after the most perfect pattern within our attainment; for character is the most powerful instrumentality within our possession. It is not so showy or noisy as wealth, or station, or fame, but it is more grand and vigorous in the silent tread of its march among human hearts. Power chiefly rests in the things that are least bustling and noisy. The world looks upon the lightning as it leaps from the cloud upon the tree, o racks and splinters it in atoms, as a strong expression of power; but not a tithe so powerful is it as that electrical vigor, which in silence spreads the earth all over with flowers, and fruits, and herbage, and holds in its still grasp the worlds that play their game of grandeur in the blue sea above us. Should a vagrant comet in mad fury burst against our earth, and jostle our planet a few feet from its century-beaten track, we should startle in gaping awe at this tremendous manifestation of power; but what would that be, compared with the silent but sleepless potency of the calm old sun who holds his retinue of worlds in serene and solemn submission, and clothes them all in annual verdure and animation?

We read that not in the earthquake that shook the mountain pillars, and waved their old bald heads among the clouds, nor yet in the whirlwind that rent the forests as gossamer, and played with the cedars of Lebanon as feathers, was God found; but in the "*still small voice*," which, like the whisper of love, breathes into the heart, what the loud word can not. So it is, the things most silent and unseen are the most powerful. Our characters are these silent sources or means of power, unseen by the visible and ambitious eye of the world, which God has permitted us to form and wield for the redemption of mankind. Let others shake the earth with an army's tread, sit on thrones, harangue in senates, or bellow from the demagogue's stump, be it mine to mold a character that God shall honor and keep unsullied in its beauty and strength, to bear about me whenever I walk among my fellows; and when eternity's light reveals the good that mortals have done, I shall have no fear that my place will not be high among the benefactors of my race.

In no other way can a man be so sure of doing good as in the formation and possession of a good character. If he gives money to a beggar, he may err in bestowing alms upon an unworthy object, who will prostitute his charity to vice. If he build a church, it may become the seat of pampered pride. If he found a college, it may in many ways fail in the good intended. So of every thing but character. An unblemished character is an evangel of a charity which nought can prevent, the ministration of a good which everywhere blesses. Not a shadow of a doubt need ever cross its possessor's mind about the good he is doing.

Such a character breathes goodness, virtue, holiness everywhere. Every one who possesses such a treasure is a benefactor of mankind. He adds to the goodness and happiness of the world. He increases its moral strength and virtue. He proves the superiority of right over wrong, of virtue over vice; and he is sowing the seeds all about him of a harvest of good, both in this world and in the spirit realm.

In the formation of a good character, every body can bless the world while they are blessing themselves, can give a glorious charity while they keep it, can impart wisdom while they obtain it, can make others rich while they are enriching themselves. While it is the best and only sure way in the world to do good unto others, it is the easiest. It requires no money, no loss of time, or sleep, or strength, but will rather add to all of these. It is so easy, that it is within every body's reach. There, perhaps, is not a youth in the country that may not thus become a public benefactor. In blessing himself with a good character, he blesses the world with a good influence and example, besides the good he does in outward acts of goodness.

It is a mistaken idea, that some people must have bad characters, that they must be demons, wretches, as by an irrevocable decree of fate. The truth is, no such decree rests upon any mortal. The decree is the very reverse of this. They were made to be clothed with beauty, to be adorned with fair characters. This is the object of their being. Not for blackness of darkness, not for vice and ruin, did the Supreme Goodness light the spark of their being. Their duty and privilege is the same as yours and mine. They have souls that should and may be clothed in respectable characters. And they have power to do it, could they but have favorable opportunities. It is easier to form a good character than a bad one. It is always pleasant to do right. It is always blessed and peaceful to be filled with pure motives.

The young heart, if left to itself, always desires to be true and generous. The natural impulse is for the good. To do evil, requires planning, contriving, and means for evading, all of which is unnatural to the heart unpracticed in evil. The child's natural inclination is to tell the truth at all times, and be dutiful and kind. He has to have many a lesson in evil from parents and associates before he becomes expert. Says a poet,

> "What a tangled web we weave,
> When first we practice to deceive

So in youth, after many lessons in evil have been taken, it is easier to do right than wrong, to form a good than a bad character. It is easier to tell the truth than a lie, to do a good than a bad act, and a thousand times more pleasant. Believe this, O youth! Good characters are easily formed, and are formed in gladness and joy; and soon formed; for the heart readily conforms to good impressions, and becomes molded by them. But bad characters are formed against positive convictions of right, in struggle and trial, in doubt and anxiety, in disquietude and foreboding fear. Bad characters are formed in a furnace of constant fire. Good ones are formed on the hills of joy.

The inducements for the formation of a good character are almost innumerable. Among these the respect of the world should not be forgotten. All people love to be respected. To obtain respect, one must possess a good character. The world respects goodness, and does it honor. No matter where it is found, in the palace or hovel, it will be respected. Every man has an inward reverence for goodness. He meets it with a feeling of awe. He pays a willing tribute to virtue. Nothing on earth is more beloved, esteemed, and honored in the world's great heart than a noble youth, one whose character is pure, whose aims are high, whose life is a moral essay. Men delight to do him good, to aid him, to give him place, preferment, office, or any thing that he may desire at their hands. Bad men will respect him. Villains will "lie low" in his presence, and assume the outward garb of good men. And they, too, will vie with each other in doing him good. It is glorious to have the unlimited confidence and respect of all who know us, and to feel that such confidence is not misplaced. It is a thought that an angel may cherish in purity. To be conscious of being beloved for our real worth, respected and honored for the excellency of our characters, is a happiness rich and hallowing in its influence.

But let the youth fix it in his mind as a fact unalterably and everlastingly true, that this respect can not be gained without a good character. He can not deceive the world with respect to his true character. It will out. And if he has deceived for awhile, he will be all the more despised when he is found out. A character stainless as truth, sweet as goodness, upright as the soul of honesty, is the only thing with which to secure and hold the world's respect.

Then, again, he wants his *own respect.* The sweetest thing in earth is self-respect. To know that one is good, is pure, is honest, is clean in the sight of God and all good men and angels, is a solid comfort that lays on the soul's bottom secure and glorious as the pillars of heaven. And though all men forsake, and slander, and abuse, it is a strength, a fortress, a rock of joy immovably sure and peaceful. Not for the world's gold, and wealth, and honors, and kingdoms would a true man sell his self-respect. For while he has this, he can not be altogether miserable, but will be happy. With a genuine, well-grounded self-respect, a man walks the earth in the dignity of a God. A dastard and a coward is he who has not self-respect.

Again, let the youth fix it as a fact that he must *make his own character*. It is a work which God has wisely consigned to him alone. No other can do it for him. Not man, or angel, or God, can form a character for his soul. These may assist him, but the work he must do himself. Character is the unseen spirit-garment that one's thoughts and feelings weave about his soul with the invisible fingers of the Divine law of reward and retribution.

It is a mysterious and glorious work, thus, with the thoughts that glow with light, and the feelings that burn with love, to weave about our souls those robes of imperishable beauty glittering with the party-colored light of every virtue which are a defense against all that can harm us, which draw around us in admiration and joy multitudes of earth's best spirits, and which, in heaven, we shall wear, unshamed by their comparison with the habiliments that mantle the angel forms. And glorious is the thought that these robes are of our own forming. They are *ours*. And the joy and the glory of their wearing is ours. Not with wealth were they bought; and not as an inherited heirloom did they descend upon us, nor as the patrimony of parental industry; not with other hands were they formed, nor with others' exertions were they obtained. No; for they are ours. We formed them by industrious exertion in behalf of the good, the beautiful, and the true; formed them in the efforts of wisdom, virtue, and love, in trial, tears, and prayer, in struggle, discipline, and hope, in constancy, energy, and devotion; and formed them for the glory of our own souls, and the good of all with whom we are linked in love and duty. We formed them for earth, and formed them for the skies. We shall wear them through time, and wear them in eternity; but, God be thanked, we may brighten and strengthen them below, and adorn and enrich them more and more, even forever in heaven.

LECTURE V.

CHOICE OF AVOCATION, AND PERSEVERANCE.

Man must Live for both Body and Mind—Temporal and Spiritual Interests not at War—Every One should have a useful Pursuit—Special Training for the Avocation—Pursuit adapted to Capacity and Taste—No Settled Business promotes Vice—What Perseverance has done—The Great in Mind are Laborious—Industry a Passport to Greatness—Friends and Success attend the Diligent—Mental and Physical Labor give Power—Nature a Scene of Labor—If you would be seen, Shine—Real Good on the Mountain-top—Idle Genius Unsuccessful—Brain, and Hand, and Nerve must Work—Life in Earnest.

In the last lecture the subject of having a fixed and determinate object in life for which to live was presented. The first and all-important object considered was the *formation of a good character*. At this time we would speak more particularly of worldly objects—objects merely temporal. Characters are formed not more in the closet of meditation and prayer, than in the busy marts of business and the fields and shops of industry. We are not altogether spirit yet, not disembodied, and hence must not forget the wants of our temporalty. Our nature in this life is compounded of spirit and matter; hence our object in life must be two-fold. We must have a spiritual and a temporal object; we must live for body and mind; and these objects must be harmonious, and act to the same end. He who prays always and labors none, prays to little purpose; he who labors always and prays none, labors to little purpose. A spiritual purpose properly pursued aids a temporal one; and a temporal purpose wisely labored for assists a spiritual one. Our temporal and spiritual objects are not at war, but in perfect and glorious harmony. For the formation of a strong and noble character, the experience of the stirring world is absolutely necessary; and for the highest and happiest success in business, such a character is necessary. We have bodies, and we must support them. It is wicked to neglect or abuse them. We are in the world, and we must live. It is practical irreverence to despise the good things of this world. To live, we must labor; must have something to do, some definite and fixed object in view, which shall be our means of support. Our moral nature requires this. An idle man can not be a moral man. A lazy, indolent do-little can not be a moral man. There is labor, strong, vigorous, nervous labor in being moral, in resisting temptation, and in doing good. It requires the highest order of action. Howard, Fenelon, Washington, Channing, were not indolent men. The truth is, Idleness is the devil's workshop, and Laziness is his master workman.

If the formation of a strong moral character is our only object, we must have before us some worldly pursuit, something in which our physical powers shall engage, some avocation, trade, profession, or calling that shall enlist our energies and fix our interests. The sooner this is fixed upon the better. Then wisdom's maxim is, *Every youth should early determine upon some life-calling, and prepare for it and pursue it with vigor.* Male and female, rich and poor, high and low, one and all, should have some honorable and useful employment, which they shall pursue as a regular business. And this should be chosen early in youth. The young energies should be directed to it, enlisted in it, and harmonized with it. The pliant powers of both the head and hand should be summoned to the work early; they will thus by early practice acquire readiness, activity, and force, which will soon become a kind of second nature. Witness the young pianist, trained in childhood to touch the sounding keys. With what ease, gracefulness, and power she presides at her obedient instrument. See the young farmer, taught in boyhood to hold the plow and swing the scythe. Not the most renowned dancer exhibits more gracefulness of motion than he. His form and all his implements obey his will, and bring forth what he asks in rich abundance.

It is the privilege and duty of man to labor, but misdirected, or labor to no definite purpose, is scarcely better than none. That labor may yield its full blessing, it must be directed to a definite and worthy object. Success in life depends much upon a fixed determination to a single point. Whoever wishes to succeed in the business affairs of life, must give the full strength of his attention and energy to his business. That this attention and energy shall produce the best results, his business should be early chosen, and his education shaped to it.

Every youth should be educated for a particular purpose and in a particular manner, which should be determined by his natural capacities and the object he has in life. But mark! *Every youth should be educated*, whatever is to be his trade or profession.

There is no honorable calling in life that may not engage the interest and attention of a whole mind, and be adorned and made attractive by the productions of a cultivated intellect.

If a young man is to follow agricultural pursuits, he should be educated for it. His education should be shaped to it. His mind should be fully trained, and its powers developed in the direction of their life pursuit. He should be made familiar with all the natural sciences, such as Chemistry, Geology, Mineralogy, Botany, and the natural history, character, and physiology of animals; for their breathing forms are all about him, and through his life he must have to do with them. His food, his drink, his dress, his all are within them and he must draw them out. The touchstone of his knowledge must be applied to their dead and living forms, that he, his wife and children, may be surrounded with the comforts and luxuries of life. With Astronomy, Physiology, mental and moral Philosophy, and the rudiments at least of a thorough mathematical education, he should be made acquainted, for these he needs every day in the care of his family and in his business transactions with the world. His course of studies, his mental training, should be directed with a wise reference to his avocation. Not only his success, but the happiness and usefulness of both himself and family, depend upon it. Again, not only his mind, but his hand, should be educated for his life's avocation.

His physical powers should be made not only strong and vigorous, but should be strictly and practically educated for his profession, so that mind and body will act together for the accomplishment of his end in life. A quack farmer is like a quack at any thing else. And an agricultural theorist unsupported by practice, is like a theorist any where, a mere puff of wind.

Similar remarks may be applied to youth who have designed to fill any of the honorable callings in which men fulfill their earthly destinies.

First of all, a choice of business should be made, and made early, with a wise reference to capacity and taste. Then the youth should be educated for it, and as much as possible in it, and when this is done, it should be pursued with an industry, energy, and enthusiasm which will warrant success.

A man or woman with no business, nothing to do, is an absolute pest to society. They are thieves, stealing that which is not theirs; beggars, eating that which they have not earned; drones, wasting the fruits of others' industry; leeches, sucking the blood of others; evil-doers, setting an example of idleness and dishonest living; hypocrites, shining in stolen and false colors; vampires, eating out the life of the community. Frown upon them, O youth. Learn in your heart to despise their course of life.

Many of our most interesting youth waste a great portion of their early life in fruitless endeavors at nothing. They have no trade, no profession, no object before them, nothing to do; and yet have a great desire to do something, and something worthy of themselves. They try this and that, and the other; offer themselves to do any thing and every thing, and yet know how to do nothing. Educate themselves they can not, for they know not what they should do it for. They waste their time, energies, and little earnings in endless changes and wanderings. They have not the stimulus of a fixed object to fasten their attention and awaken their energies; not a known prize to win. They wish for good things, but have no way to attain them; desire to be useful, but little means for being so. They lay plans, invent schemes, form theories, build castles, but never stop to execute and realize them. Poor creatures! All that ails them is the want of an object—a *single object.* They look at a hundred, and see nothing. If they should look steadily at one, they would see it distinctly. They grasp at random at a hundred things and catch nothing. It is like shooting among a scattered flock of pigeons. The chances are doubtful. This will never do—no, never. Success, respectability, and happiness are found in a permanent business. An early choice of some business, devotion to it, and preparation for it, should be made by every youth.

When the two objects, business and character, as the great end of life, are fairly before a youth, what then? Why, he must attain those objects. Will wishes and prayers bring them into his hands? By no means. He must work as well as wish, labor as well as pray. His hand must be as stout as his heart, his arm as strong as his head. Purpose must be followed by action, words by blows And these must be repeated "from morn till night, from youth till hoary age." "Continual dropping wears a stone." So persevering labor gains our objects. Perseverance is the virtue wanted, a lion-hearted purpose of victory. It is this that builds, constructs, accomplishes whatever is great, good, and valuable.

Perseverance built the pyramids on Egypt's plains, erected the gorgeous temple at Jerusalem, reared the seven-hilled city, inclosed in adamant the Chinese empire, scaled the stormy, cloud-capped Alps, opened a highway through the watery wilderness of the Atlantic, leveled the forests of a new world, and reared in its stead a community of states and nations. It has wrought from the marble block the exquisite creations of genius, painted on the canvas the gorgeous mimicry of nature, and engraved on metallic surface the viewless substance of the shadow. It has put in motion millions of spindles, winged as many flying shuttles, harnessed a thousand iron steeds to as many freighted cars, and set them flying from town to town and nation to nation, tunneled mountains of granite and annihilated space with the lightning's speed. It has whitened the waters of the world with the sails of a hundred nations, navigated every sea and explored every land. It has reduced nature in her thousand forms to as many sciences, taught her laws, prophesied her future movements, measured her untrodden spaces, counted her myriad hosts of worlds, and computed their distances, dimensions, and velocities.

But greater still are the works of perseverance in the world of mind. What are the productions of science and art compared with the splendid achievements won in the human soul? What is a monument of constructive genius, compared with the living domes of thought, the sparkling temples of virtue, and the rich, glory-wreathed sanctuaries of religion, which perseverance has wrought out and reared in the souls of the good? What are the toil-sweated productions of wealth piled in vast profusion around a Gerard, or a Rothschild, when weighed against the stores of wisdom, the treasures of knowledge, and the strength, beauty, and glory with which this victorious virtue has enriched and adorned a great multitude of minds during the march of a hundred generations? How little can we tell, how little know, the brain-sweat, the heart-labor, the conscience-struggles which it cost to make a Newton, a Howard, or a Channing; how many days of toil, how many nights of weariness, how many months and years of vigilant, powerful effort, was spent to perfect in them what the world has bowed to in reverence. Their words have a power, their names a charm, and their deeds a glory. How came this wealth of soul to be theirs? Why are their names watchwords of power set high on the temple of fame? Why does childhood lisp them in reverence, and age feel a thrill of pleasure when they are mentioned?

They were the sons of Perseverance—of unremitting industry and toil. They were once as weak and helpless as any of us—once as destitute of wisdom, virtue, and power as any infant. Once the very alphabet of that language which they have wielded with such magic effect, was unknown to them. They toiled long to learn it, to get its sounds, understand its dependencies, and longer still to obtain the secret of its highest charm and mightiest power, and yet even longer for those living, glorious thoughts which they bade it bear to an astonished and admiring world. Their characters, which are now given to the world, and will be to millions yet unborn, as patterns of greatness and goodness, were made by that untiring perseverance which marked their whole lives. From childhood to age they knew no such word as fail. Defeat only gave them power; difficulty only taught them the necessity of redoubled exertions; dangers gave them courage; the sight of great labors inspired in them corresponding exertions. So it has been with all men and all women who have been eminently successful in any profession or calling in life. Their success has been wrought out by persevering industry. Successful men owe more to their perseverance than to their natural powers, their friends, or the favorable circumstances around them. Genius will falter by the side of labor; great powers will yield to great industry. Talent is desirable, but perseverance is more so. It will make mental powers, or, at least, it will strengthen those already made. Yes, it will make mental power. The most available and successful kind of mental power is that made by the hand of cultivation.

It will also make friends. Who will not befriend the persevering, energetic youth, the fearless man of industry? Who is not a friend to him who is a friend to himself? He who perseveres in business, and hardships, and discouragements, will always find ready and generous friends in every time of need. He who perseveres in a course of wisdom, rectitude, and benevolence, is sure to gather around him friends who will be true and faithful. Honest industry will procure friends in any community and any part of the civilized world. Go to the men of business, of worth, of influence, and ask them who shall have their confidence and support. They will tell you, the men who falter not by the wayside, who toil on in their callings against every barrier, whose eye is bent upward, and whose motto is "Excelsior." These are the men to whom they give their confidence. But they shun the lazy, the indolent, the fearful, and faltering. They would as soon trust the wind as such men. If you would win friends, be steady and true to yourself; be the unfailing friend of your own purposes, stand by your own character, and others will come to your aid. Though the earth quake and the heavens gather blackness, be true to your course and yourself. Quail not, nor doubt of the result; victory will be yours. Friends will come. A thousand arms of strength will be bared to sustain you.

First, be sure that your trade, your profession, your calling in life is a good one—one that God and goodness sanctions; then be true as steel to it. Think for it, plan for it, work for it, live for it; throw in your mind, might, strength, heart, and soul into your actions for it, and success will crown you her favored child. No matter whether your object be great or small, whether it be the planting of a nation or a patch of potatoes, the same perseverance is necessary. Every body admires an iron determination, and comes to the aid of him who directs it to good.

But perseverance will not only make friends, but it will make favorable circumstances. It will change the face of all things around us. It is silly and cowardly to complain of the circumstances that are against us. Clouds of darkness, evil forebodings, opposition, enemies, barriers of every kind, will vanish before a stout heart and resolute energy of soul. The Alps stood between Napoleon and Italy, which he desired to conquer. He scaled the mountain and descended upon his prey. His startling descent more than half conquered the country. He forced every circumstance into his favor. His greatest barrier proved a sure means of victory. A conquered enemy is often the readiest slave. So a barrier once scaled affords a vantage-ground for our future efforts. Opposing circumstances often create strength, both mental and physical. Labor makes us strong. Opposition gives us greater power of resistance. To overcome one barrier gives us greater ability to overcome the next. It is cowardice to grumble about circumstances. Some men always talk as though fate had woven a web of circumstances against them, and it is useless for them to try to break through it. Out upon such dastardly whining! It is their business to dash on in pursuit of their object against every thing. Then circumstances will gradually turn in their favor, and they will deem themselves the favored children of destiny.

Look at Nature. She has a voice, which is the voice of God, teaching a thousand lessons of perseverance. The lofty mountains are wearing down by slow degrees. The ocean is gradually, but slowly, filling up, by deposits from its thousand rivers. The Niagara Falls have worn back several miles through the hard limestone, over which it pours its thundering columns of water, and will by-and-by drain the great lake which feeds its boiling chasm. The Red Sea and whole regions of the Pacific Ocean are gradually filling up by the labors of a little insect, so small as to be almost invisible to the naked eye. These stupendous works are going on before our eyes, by a slow but sure process. They teach a great lesson of perseverance. Nature has but one voice on this subject, that is "persevere." God has but one voice, that is "persevere," and duty proclaims the same lesson. More depends upon an active perseverance than upon genius. Says a common-sense author upon this subject, "Genius, unexerted, is no more genius than a bushel of acorns is a forest of oaks." There may be epics in men's brains, just as there are oaks in acorns, but the tree and the bark must come out before we can measure them. We very naturally recall here that large class of grumblers and wishers, who spend their time in longing to be higher than they are, while they should have been employed to advance themselves. These bitterly moralize on the injustice of society. Do they want a change? Let them then change! Who prevents them? If you are as high as your faculties will permit you to rise in the scale of society, why should you complain of men?

It is God that arranged the law of precedence. Implead

Him or be silent! If you have capacity for a higher station, take it. What hinders you? How many men would love to go to sleep beggars, and wake up Rothschilds or Astors? How many would fain go to bed dunces, to be waked up Solomons? You reap what you have sown. Those who have sown dunce-seed, vice-seed, laziness-seed, usually get a crop. They that sow the wind reap a whirlwind. A man of mere "capacity undeveloped" is only an organized degradation with a shine on it. A flint and a genius that will not strike fire are no better than wet junk-wood. We have Scripture for it, that "A living dog is better than a dead lion!" If you would go up, go—if you would be seen, shine. At the present day eminent position, in any profession, is the result of hard, unwearied labor. Men can no longer fly at one dash into eminent position. They have got to hammer it out by steady and rugged blows. The world is no longer clay, but rather iron, in the hands of its workers.

Work is the order of this day. The slow penny is surer than the quick dollar. The slow trotter will out-travel the fleet racer. Genius darts, flutters, and tires; but perseverance wears and wins. The all-day horse wins the race. The afternoon man wears off the laurels. The last blow finishes the nail.

Men must learn to labor and to wait, if they would succeed. Brains grow by use as well as hands. The greatest man is the one who uses his brains the most, who has added most to his natural stock of power. Would you have fleeter feet? Try them in the race. Would you have stronger minds? Put them at rational thinking. They will grow strong by action. Would you have greater success? Use greater and more rational and con stant efforts? Does competition trouble you? Work away; what is your competitor but a man? Are you a coward, that you shrink from the contest? Then you ought to be beaten. Is the end of your labors a long way off? Every step takes you nearer to it. Is it a weary distance to look at? Ah, you are faint-hearted! That is the trouble with the multitude of youth. Youth are not so lazy as they are cowardly. They may bluster at first, but they won't "stick it out." Young farmer, do you covet a homestead, nice and comfortable, for yourself and that sweet one of your day-dreams? What hinders that you should not have it? Persevering industry, with proper economy, will give you the farm. A man can get what he wants if he is not faint-hearted.

Youth, learn this lesson: *All real good is on the mount-ain-top—you must go up there to get it.* The greater the good, the higher the mount which it crowns; and the longer and greater the efforts necessary to secure it.

Would you secure to yourself a high, noble, Christian character? It is found on the mount of self-denial and prayer. Go up then hastily, cheerily, and thankfully, heeding not the allurements by the way-side, and soon you will be arrayed in the gorgeous object of your noble ambition. You have but to do as did Christ every day you live, be prayerful and active in goodness. Sow the seeds of every virtue in your heart, and warm the soil with the sunlight of wisdom. Do as others have done, work long and well. Bridle the tongue; curb the passions; check the appetites; restrain the propensities; master the will; subdue the impulses; conquer the spirit of evil. Be sleepless, watchful, ever active, and you will not, can not fail. Fail! Fail is not in the persevering man's vocabulary. Whether it is fame, fortune, competency, professional success, learning, the good of others, a single virtue, or the constellated union of all virtues that you seek, there is but one way to obtain it: it is by persevering effort.

Great natural endowments are desirable, but perseverance is better. Perseverance must attend these, or there can be no success. The common mind with perseverance will outstrip the most godlike genius without it. Genius may make a few glorious leaps. Like a blazing meteor it may flash half across the horizon at once. But the common mind, led on by its faithful guide, perseverance, though it may lag behind for a season, will finally march on, gaining speed with time, and will leave genius worn out and discouraged amid its own faded glories. When the boy cut his way with his pocket-knife up the almost perpendicular abutment of the Natural Bridge, and left his companions behind gazing in wonder and astonishment at him as he ascended, as if by miracle, toward the top of that dark defile, two hundred feet in depth, he did it not by virtue of any superior strength or capacity, but only by dint of perseverance. Hole by hole he cut in the rock; step by step he ascended. His eye was bent upward, and upward he went, to enroll his name among those of the brave and daring boys whose souls were fired with the spirit of perseverance. So it is with every youth. If he persevere, she goes up. Each step lifts him higher. Each effort moves him onward. Each blow makes a hole for his feet. Continual struggle, unremitted effort, is the only hope. Toil is the price of success. Learn it, young farmer, mechanic, student, minister, physician, Christian. Learn it, ye formers of character, ye followers of Christ, ye would-be men and women. Ye must have something to do, and do it with all your might. Ye must harden your hands and sweat your brains. Ye must work your nerves and strain your sinews. Ye must be at it, and always at it. No trembling, doubting, hesitating, flying the track. Like the boy on the rock, ye can not go back. Onward ye must go. There is a great work for ye all to do, a deep and earnest life-work, solemn, real, and useful. Life is no idle game, no farce to amuse and be forgotten. It is a fixed and stern reality, fuller of duties than the sky is of stars.

Every moment has a three-fold duty—one to yourself, your fellow, and your God. Life's great end ye should labor to reach. Youth is the time to begin the struggle. A great American poet has breathed into a stirring poem the spirit with which all youth should be fired. Let us read it and close.

Tell me not in mournful numbers,
  Life is but an empty dream!
For the soul is dead that slumbers,
  And things are not what they seem.

Life is real! Life is earnest!
  And the grave is not its goal;
Dust thou art; to dust returnest,
  Was not spoken of the soul.

Not enjoyment and not sorrow
  Is our destined end or way;
But to act that each to-morrow
  Find us farther than to day.

Art is long, and time is fleeting,
  And our hearts, though stout and brave,
Still like muffled drums are beating
  Funeral marches to the grave.

In the world's broad field of battle,
  In the bivouac of life,
Be not like dumb, driven cattle,
  Be a hero in the strife.

Trust no fortune, however pleasant!
  Let the dead Past bury its dead!
Act, act in the living Present,
  Heart within and God o'erhead!

Lives of great men all remind us
  We can make our lives sublime,
And departing leave behind us
  Footprints on the sands of time.

Footprints that perhaps another
  Sailing o'er life's solemn main,
A forlorn and shipwrecked brother,
  Seeing, shall take heart again.

Let us then be up and doing,
  With a heart for any fate;
Still achieving, still pursuing,
  Learn to labor and to wait.—LONGFELLOW.

LECTURE VI.

HEALTH.

Health the Foundation of all Successful Action—Bright Stars oftenest Eclipsed—Health a Binding Duty—Omniscience of the Eye—Omnipotence of the Hand—Disease makes Man a Blank—Natural Death Rare—Disease a Penalty, not a Curse—Health a Duty to Friends and to God—We Daily Sin against Ourselves—Prevention the Best Doctor—All Else rather than Health Studied—Disease Disgraceful—Ignorance the Mother of Disease—Youth the Hope of the World—How to Preserve Health.

In previous lectures, I have spoken of the objects of life and of perseverance, as requisite, or necessary, to their attainment. But it is very clear that there are many other things which must accompany perseverance, or no thing will be effected. In this lecture it is my purpose to speak of one of these prerequisites to perseverance, and consequently, to success in life; that prerequisite is *Health.*

Nothing is clearer than that the most towering genius, the most determined ambition, the most untiring perseverance, must be all unavailing in the struggle for life's great objects without health. Genius may plume her wings for a lofty flight, may revel among her own brilliant creations, may bathe her plumage in the glittering light of the stars; if young health stand not by her side, to give strength to her pinions, energy and permanency to her young and daring powers, she will be compelled to come down even to the earth, and, like a young eagle struck on his first upward flight by the huntsman's ball, flutter in the dust, a crippled, broken, miserable thing of life in the arms of death.

What more truly heart-rending sight, than to witness a youth, with noble aspirations and lofty powers, with thoughts all great and pure, and feelings that breathe of angel strength and beauty, whose whole soul is given up to God and goodness, and in every chamber of which beams the light of truth and heaven, cut slowly down by the ruthless hand of disease, in the very hour when the promise is fairest, and the hope and the love of friends are brightest and strongest. If there is any thing that should cause the earth to weep, and the cold world to clothe its heart in weeds of mourning, it is the loss of such spirits. They are the suns and stars that shine in this world's firmament; they are the gold, diamonds, and flowers that enrich and beautify its homes, its altars, its seats of justice, its asylums of charity, and its halls of learning. They save it from ruin, and redeem it from the grasp of moral death. And yet it is ours to witness often the departure of such angel spirits. They go from us, and a region of darkness is left around us, as when a sun goes out in the heavens, or a star falls, to leave its place forever dark. Disease will cripple the mightiest energies, enervate the strongest intellect, unnerve the most stalwart arm, and blight the fairest prospects. Truly can we say that health is the first prerequisite to success in the true objects of life. It is the *one thing* without which nothing can be effected. It is the absolute essential to the performance of man's proper duties; that without which he can perform no duty properly; that without which he can neither be useful to himself, his fellow, or his God; can neither be intellectual, moral, or religious. Yes; health is the great boon which all should crave, the right arm of every power, both of body and soul, the buckler of the head, and the shield of the heart.

Permit me to read you the opinion of a great divine upon this subject. He says: "This may be thought by some a singular topic to introduce in a course of lectures from the pulpit, and upon the Sabbath; but I regard the preservation of health as an important and binding duty. God has made us denizens of this earth. He has clothed our better and immortal nature in a material vesture, and linked us by physical bonds to the animal creation. And wonderful is the mechanism by which He has adapted us to this sphere, intimately is the soul connected with it! Wonderful are the existences which He has created upon the relations of action and reaction of cause and effect. Has He filled this vast nature, this universe of ocean, earth, and air, with music, making it, as it were, one great organ, with its stops and valves of varied melody, and all its living and harmonious voices? So has He tuned the ear to hear it all, molding it in perfect shape, and giving it chords to vibrate with delight. Untune these chords, clog these delicate avenues of sound, and are you not going counter to the manifest design of God? Are you not breaking an express law, and therefore sinning? See how true it is, that God has made the world not only useful, but beautiful. He has not only made the sky, but He has given it the softest color of the prism. He has not only hung the stars there, but He has made them to sparkle gloriously all athwart that high blue dome. He not only condenses the vapors into clouds, but they brighten in gorgeous hues around the sun, or darken in grandeur beneath the storm. He has not only given the springs 'to run among the hills,' but He sprinkles their water-drops on high and abroad, until they throw an arc across the abyss, and glitter in the indescribable beauty of the rainbow. And the earth is clothed with greenness and flowers, and the mountains lift their battlements, and ocean spreads out its majesty. Look abroad, and see how beauty blends with usefulness in the multitude of created things. And what is there in man adapted to all this? That tender and delicate organ the eye—paralyze its delicate nerves, quench its light, seal up its lids, and all this enchantment, this field of glorious vision, disappears. Is it not a duty, then, to nourish and preserve this portion of the human frame? Look at the *hand*—a little organ, but how curiously wrought! How manifold and necessary are its functions! What an agent has it been for the wants and designs of man! The *hand*—what would the mind be without it? How has it molded and made palpable the conceptions of that mind, removed its obstacles, and gone before it to pioneer its progress! The *hand*—it wrought the statue of Memnon, and hung the brazen gates of Thebes; it fixed the mariner's trembling needle upon its axis, and first heaved back the tremendous bar of the printing-press. It opened the tubes for Galileo, until world after world swept largely before his vision; and it reefed the high top-sail that rustled over Columbus in the morning breezes of Bahamas. And it has held the sword with which freedom has fought her battles; it has poised the axe of the dauntless woodman, as he opened the paths of civilization; it turned the mystic leaves upon which Milton and Shakspeare inscribed their burning thoughts; and it secured, finally, the pen that signed the Declaration of Independence. Would you weaken the hand, then? Would you make it nerveless or useless? If so, would you not break a great physical law of the Creator's own ordaining? You perceive the importance of preserving the health of the body in *all* its organs and functions. For if these important portions are to be cherished, so are the minor powers. They are necessary to carrying out the designs of our existence; they are necessary to doing good; they are necessary to effect the ideas of mind; as is their condition, so, often, is this higher and nobler principle."

Then am I not justified in making *health* the subject of a lecture, and in urging its claims most earnestly upon the young? Most surely no subject is more worthy of our serious consideration, considered morally or religiously. It is just as much a duty to preserve health, as to love our neighbor, or worship God; and just as surely a sin to violate the laws of health, as to lie, cheat, steal, murder, or blaspheme the name of the Most High. God has laid upon us great and important duties; duties which it is impossible for us to perform without health and its consequent strength of body and mind.

The performance of these duties depend upon the possession of health. Now, if we destroy our health, or violate the laws by which we hold it, we destroy our ability to perform our God-given duties. And it amounts to just the same as though we had retained the health, and refused to perform our duties. If a father should give his child a glass, and ask him to bring him a glass of water, and the child should break the glass through a reckless stupidity and carelessness, and then came and very innocently plead that he could not bring the water, because the glass had fallen to pieces, he would be slow to receive the boy's excuse as a valid one. The father would justly hold him accountable for breaking the glass and the non-performance of his duty.

Our Father has laid important duties upon us, and given us health by which we are enabled to perform these duties. Now, if we injure our health, or violate the laws by which we hold it, so as to render it impossible for us to perform what is required of us, He will hold us accountable both for the injury to our health and the non-performance of our duties. It is just about impossible for any man to perform the duties of life with pain in every joint, and misery in every portion of his body. So intimate is the connection between the body and the mind, that the mind can neither think right nor feel right, when the body is sickly, nervous, diseased, and in pain. Its judgment must be impaired, its sense of right blunted, its perceptions modified and deranged by the disease. Neither can it feel patient, kind, forbearing, forgiving, and charitable, as when in health. Its affections will be weakened, its benevolence enervated, and its religious aspirations all distracted and broken. It can neither love man, nor worship God, nor cultivate its own powers with its full force, without the aid of health. I remarked that it is just as surely a sin to destroy health as to murder. And I might have said that the violation of the laws of health is murder. Disease is the procuring cause of death in almost every instance. There is probably not one in a hundred of our race that dies a natural death. Nearly all are murdered, not suddenly, but by slow degrees, by continual, life-long violations of physical and organic laws, by violations more numerous than the hairs on our heads. There is no doubt that the proper age of man is cut short more than one half, and that half that is lived, is not more than half lived; so that we live out not more than one quarter of the life we ought to live, and this three quarters is cut off by violations of laws with which we may be perfectly familiar, and with which we may comply. Go into your graveyards, and read the ages of the young whose bodies lie buried there, and behold the graves but a few spans long, then ask yourselves if violated health is not murder. I would that people everywhere could be made to view this subject in its proper light—I mean in a moral light; could feel as morally bound to preserve their health, as to be honest or religious; could feel that it is an absolute and positive sin to violate a single physical or organic law of their being. The truth is, many people look upon sickness as a sort of scourge or visitation sent by God, which can not be avoided, and which must be submitted to with as good a grace as possible. Now, if sickness is a scourge from God, sin is just as much so. If we can avoid one, we can the other. One is a violation of the moral law; the other is occasioned by a violation of both a physical and moral law. It is true sickness is a scourge sent from God; but it is for our transgressions of His physical laws. If we will live in obedience to His laws, He will not send the scourge. We ought to look upon sickness and sin in the same light, and with the same feelings. They should both be regarded as within our control, and subject to the dictations of our wills. It is true, there are accidents which we can not control, and causes of disease beyond our immediate reach. But these are the *exceptions*, and not the general rule. People may be healthy and well, if they will; if they will try as hard as they do to get what they call the *good* things of this world, which not unfrequently are the bad things.

There is one other consideration of a moral nature which I wish to notice before leaving this part of the subject. In viewing the moral obligations to preserve health, we should not lose sight of the fact that these bodies, not only fearfully and wonderfully, but beautifully made, are the gifts of our Father. He made them, He gave them, He contrived them, He decorated them, and added a glow of pleasure and a thrill of joy to the healthy action of each and every portion. The health which they naturally possess, is His gift; and if we respect Him properly, if our hearts duly appreciate His favors, and rise in grateful thanksgivings to Him, we shall surely strive to preserve our bodies in their original beauty and strength, and present these continually before Him in an associated glow of health, activity, and power. When we neglect, or abuse these homes which He has provided for our spirit's earthly dwelling-places, we fail in gratitude to Him, and are guilty of sin in His sight, of practical irreverence to Him.

Once more. If we feel properly those thrilling emotions of friendship and love which should glow in every true heart toward its friends, these ought to prompt to obedience to the laws of health. For how unhappy will our sickness make our friends! How keen is their sorrow when they see us languishing on beds of disease, when they see our bodies writhing in pain, and our whole beings racked with torture and agony. When the truly good suffer and die from bodily disease, their friends are the most intense sufferers; for theirs is the agony of broken hearts, of bleeding sympathies. This thought ought to awaken us to the most vigilant and untiring efforts to preserve and perfect that health that belongs to us, that gift of our Father's love. All the duties we owe to ourselves, our friends, and country, our race, and our God, depend upon health for their performance, as well as our own happiness. Every consideration of a moral nature assures us that we are morally bound to preserve health, as much as to obey any of the mandates of the moral law. But how poorly the people of this world heed this moral obligation. Look around you for that rare thing, that anomaly in the earth, a healthy person, one whose blood bounds through his veins bearing the vermillion of health, one whose lip is parched never with a fever's flaw, whose breath is sweet as the fragrance of a new-blown rose, whose step is as elastic as that of the forest roe, whose frame is erect and full, whose sleep is sweet, and whose days and nights are free from pain. Ah, where will you find such an one? And yet this is a picture of what we all should be, regarded in a physical light.

Very few are to be found who have no disease about them, no diseased members, no weak spots, no open doors asking disease to walk in. And well may it be so. The wonder is not that people are so sickly, but that they are so well. If their frames were not made stronger than iron and tougher than any known substance, they would not, could not, live any length of time; for nearly all of us live in almost continual transgression of the laws of vital economy. We eat unwholesome food, improper quantities, and at improper times; we drink unwholesome drinks, and are intemperate in these; we breathe impure air, often air impregnated with the very seeds of death; we sleep frequently in small and almost always in confined rooms, as though we regarded the pure air of heaven as dangerous; we often sleep when we should be awake, and are awake when we should be asleep; we often clothe ourselves in attire illy adapted to the free development and action of the muscular powers; we often take too violent

and severe exercise, and often not enough; we expose ourselves to a thousand dangers, and confine ourselves when the hill-air should fan our brows and invigorate our spirits; we have a thousand evil and intemperate habits, a hundredth part of which I have not time nor inclination now to mention. And this is the way we do from infancy onward; continually transgressing, and continually suffering, and about as continually doctoring. The drugs that many people take are enough to undermine the stoutest constitutions. The course pursued by about half of the world, might be well described by this "see-saw," *get sick and take drugs, get sick and take drugs.*

Drugs are proper enough in their place, but their place is not often in the human stomach, and even though they may be necessary to cure a disease, it is not as necessary that that disease should exist. We should study prevention more than cure. Let physicians study cures. The "Materia Medica" is in their hands, and let them keep it. The less we have to do with it, the better, if we are wise, so as not to need its remedies. But let *us* study *prevention*, study the laws of health, the laws of our being, and learn to obey them as a moral duty of the first importance.

But here again how remiss are we. How little do we know of ourselves, of the buildings in which we dwell, of the laws by which they exist, and the means necessary to keep them in repair. And how little do we care about this knowledge which we so much need. How few there are, especially among the young, who know comparatively

any thing about their own systems, or about the laws which govern their health. This is the last kind of knowledge which people seek. Go into our people's houses, and examine their libraries, and you will find books on history, books on law, books on physiology, books on theology and religion, books on agriculture and mechanism, books on law, and war, and murder, tales, and poems, and lectures, and every thing but books on the human system, treating of the laws which govern health. You will find long treatises on diseases and the medicines necessary to cure them, on calomel and jalap, lobelia and pepper, on allopathy, homeopathy, and hydropathy, as applied to working wonders in curing all incurable diseases, and raising men almost from the dead; but no treatises showing the application of these various systems to the preservation of health. The last book in nearly all libraries is a book on physiology, applying its instructions to the preservation of health. And into most family libraries it is yet to be introduced. Read our papers, periodicals, journals, registers, and you will find all subjects treated but the one under consideration. Go into our schools and colleges, and you will be surprised to find only here and there a youth making any effort to make himself acquainted with himself or the laws which govern his health. Every thing else, all other sciences, are studied; languages on which the mold of ages has gathered, are poured over for years, and sciences as dry and impracticable as can well be imagined, are made the subjects of long and intense interest, while the most important study of practical physiology is entirely neglected. People act as though they thought every thing else more necessary than health; and at times they seem tc act as though they thought it a virtue to be sick. Why are all people so unacquainted with themselves; so ignorant of the laws and actions of their own systems? It seems to me almost unaccountable. What study is more delightful, more intensely interesting, than human physiology. Nothing can be more so. Upon our knowledge of this depends our ability to preserve health, and to perfect the various powers of the system.

But something more than simple knowledge is necessary. We must feel a determination to abide by the dictates of that knowledge, to be controlled by its voice. We must make a practical use of what we learn and what we know, reduce it to practice in every-day life. We should look upon it as a religious duty, not less sacred and imperious than any other we have to perform. We are ashamed of our sins, and try to hide them from the world. When we deceive, lie, cheat, or steal, we seek to conceal our wickedness from the eye of our fellows. We are ashamed of it. We ought to be just as much ashamed of our diseases, of our corruptions of body; for they are both transgressions of the laws of God, which we are under the highest moral obligations to obey. Our consciences should rebuke us just as severely for being sick, as for being wicked; for both unfit us alike for the performance of our duties to God and man. If we would be truly virtuous, upright, and moral, if we would fulfill the whole laws of God, if we would reap the fullest enjoyments of life, if we would live in the nearest proximity to perfection, if we would stand in a moral point of view before God blameless, we should seek for both physical and moral health. It should be our most continual study to be pure, bodily and spiritually.

It is not my purpose in this lecture to attempt to point out the course of life necessary to health, so much as to present the moral obligations we are under to preserve the health of our physical beings. To me it is a religious duty, scarcely inferior to any other. And although for it I may receive the jeers and taunts of my fellows, it is still a duty which, under God, I must strive to perform, and seek to induce others to do the same. And if I could by any means induce my young friends to give this subject the study, the reflection, the investigation that its importance demands, I should feel that I had done a service which will add much to their happiness and usefulness in life. The first thing that young people want upon this subject is enlightenment, knowledge, physiological knowledge, a knowledge of themselves, a knowledge of what is necessary to their physical well-being. And secondly, a determination to abide by the teachings of that knowledge.

To the young I address myself upon this subject with far more confidence than to those who have passed the meridian of life. The older people are so thoroughly fixed, so deeply rooted, and so interwoven with strong and bitter prejudices, and such a blind devotion to custom, or the old way, that they may about as well be given over to hardness of heart and blindness of mind, as to attempt to reform them. But the habits of the young are less firmly fixed. Their minds are more open to conviction. They have longer lives before them, and higher aspirations within them. They have more to live for and more to do; and more to induce them to strive for the straight and narrow path of life. Upon the youth we must rely chiefly for all we hope for the world and humanity. And hence to them I present this subject, with some degree of confidence that they will be benefited by it. I should be glad to see every youth more familiar with his own system than the geography of his father's farm or homestead; to see all know as much about themselves as any school book; and be familiar with the actions of every part of their systems, and the influences of air, exercise, diet, sleep, exposure, intemperance, etc., etc. If they were thus acquainted with themselves, they might avoid many of the rocks and quicksands upon which others have stranded. And the very fact of striving to conform to the laws of health, would teach them a lesson of obedience which they would strive to carry out in all the walks of life. People's knowledge must always be far in advance of their obedience. They *know* better than they *do*. Even now nearly all people *know* how to take much better care of their health than they *do*. They transgress many known laws, disobey a thousand known injunctions. So it will always be in this world. Knowledge must be far in advance of obedience. But as knowledge increases, obedience will increase. Give new instruction, and, to a certain extent, they will follow it. Then let knowledge increase. Let wisdom abound.

Let the teacher go forth. Let the pupils be many. Yea let all become students, and seek to familiarize themselves with their own wonderful natures. Let every home be made a study. Let every sitting-room table have on it an open book of physiological instruction. Let every library be well supplied with books on this subject. Let every room be hung around with charts. Let all young people at home and at school have daily lessons on health. And let all study the operations of their own systems, make experiments for themselves, and determine what is best for their own health. Systems differ a little. No absolute rule can be laid down for all to follow which would be of the highest practicable benefit to all. But the differences are small. The general laws of health are universal. Let all seek the general laws of health, and the minute differences they will easily find out. Let youth remember the long life that is before them, remember the great duties that devolve upon them, what they are, and what they ought to be, and then decide whether they will strive to be healthy and strong, free from disease, pain, physical debility and corruptions, that they may be and do what God, humanity, and their own happiness and well-being ask of them.

LECTURE VII.

TEMPERANCE.

A Deceitful Sea of Pleasure—Danger unconsciously Near—Elements of Intemperance within Us—Save the Image of God from Blight—Bodily Pains preach Temperance—What is Intemperance—A Personal Test of Intemperance—Appetite, a Voice of Warning—Drunkards not the only Intemperate—Rich Tables the Bane of Temperance—Little Roots support the Main Trunk—Youth the Seed-ground of Wheat or Tares—Ultimate Effects of Temperance.

HE who stands upon the watch-tower of virtue should be faithful to give the alarm of danger when it is near. It should be sounded when the engulfing pool is yet in the distance, and the danger easily avoided. This duty too long neglected, and all is lost.

He who is upon the present watch beholds a perilous scene before him. It is a maelstrom, dark, whirling, yawning. It is roaring with wrecks, groans, and horrid ruin of fortunes and lives. It is named *Intemperance*, and is situated in the very center of the great sea of pleasure. The waters which form this ruinous pool come in from every direction. They come not rushing and foaming, but with a gradual and gentle flow. So smoothly do they glide, that those who are riding upon their waves are scarcely ever aware that they are moving toward the pool. The waters break into scarcely perceptible ripples, long before they reach the sloping chasm, into which they plunge with awful fury. The descent to it is so gentle as to be scarcely perceptible without the closest observation. Long may the thoughtless pleasure-seeker glide upon these waters, not dreaming that his bark is descending the rippling slope of danger. The sea is bright and beautiful; and it looks to the inexperienced mariner even more so down the rippling descent. The starry gleams of the breaking waters invite him thither. Their glancing light attracts his gaze, and wins a desire to sail amid its varied and changing beauties. This variety adds a new desire, this desire produces excitement, and this excitement bewilders judgment and stimulates to misguided actions.

Thus, without being aware of danger, he glides at first slowly down, and then faster and still faster down, till the waters break into foam, and envelop him in a cloud of darkness, in the midst of which he is hurried on, and still on, to ruin. Thus is this fascinating sea of pleasure spread around the engulfing pool of intemperance, sloping in from every direction, inviting and still inviting its voyagers to sail down its danger-strewn declivities. Not one path alone leads to this sullen gulf of woe; not one only current, as too many have supposed, hurries down this dark abyss; but all around, on every side, the waters tend downward. There are a thousand currents leading in. Some, it is true, are more rapid than others. Some rush in quickly, and bear down all who ride upon their waters to quick and certain ruin.

Others glide more slowly, but none the less surely, to the same end. The streams of intemperance are legion.

The allurements that lead downward are equally numerous. Every appetite, lust, passion, and feeling holds out various allurements to intemperate indulgence. There is not a power of the mind, affection of the heart, nor animal desire, that may not dispose to some form of intemperance, which may injure the body or paralyze the energies of the mind. All forms of intemperance are evil, and destroy some function of body or mind, some member or faculty, the disease of which spreads in harmony through the whole. The dangers from this source are imminent and fearful, and spread on every hand.

In former lectures the subjects of health of body and mind have been considered. We may now consider temperance as absolutely essential to both.

A great poet has said:

> "Reason's whole pleasure, all the joys of sense,
> Lie in these words, *health, peace*, and *competence;*
> But *health* consists in *temperance* alone,
> And *peace*, O virtue! peace is all thy own."

Health consists in temperance. This is the truth, this is the law, primary and essential, which every youth should know. Know! Yes, know by heart. It should be written on every leaf and every living thing. Yea, it is written on all that lives and moves. Animals, birds, fishes, vegetables—all are temperate but man, and all full of rosy health but him. Will you not read it, O Youth! this law of temperance

See, thy cheek has a rose upon it, health's blushing picture. Will you preserve it, to adorn the face of age? Thy step is elastic. Will you retain its elastic tread, to bear the rugged frame of a strong maturity, and give thy latter years this cheerful legacy? Beauty is thine. Wilt thou let it dwell about thee, even till the snow-fall of thy winter whitens thy head? Dost thou prize these gifts, which the good hand of thy Father hath bestowed upon thy youth? Tell the world how well you prize them by obeying the law by which they are preserved. That law is temperance. It is written in the statute-book of your bodies and minds. Will you read it, will you learn it? Its principles are simple and plain. You can be as wise upon them as any scholar, physician, or philosopher. You have all the great teachers of temperance in and about you. You have stom achs, brains, nerves, bones, sinews, and muscles. You have mind, reason, conscience, affection. You have friends, country, and home. You have interests, hopes, and life. You have all the great ends and aims of a human being to accomplish. You have God, his Son, and Gospel. You have all that is true in thought, beautiful in life, and glorious in hope. All these are teachers of temperance. They all exhort you to a temperate mode of life. What more do you wish—what more can you ask? They all give you daily lectures upon temperance. You have every thing—all the living voices of God, all His teachers, preachers, most eloquent expounders of truth and duty, reading you perpetual lectures on temperance. Surely the fault is yours if you do not heed them. Every thing bids you be temperate in all things—temperate in the gratification of your appetites, temperate in your pleasures, labors, desires, amusements, hopes, actions, yea, in every possible way.

When you have returned late at night from a pleasure party or frolic, and after an honr or two of feverish sleep, you have risen worn and weary, and out-of-sorts, have you not understood the lecture which your jaded body was then reading you? It run thus: "Be more temperate in your amusements; give me sleep and rest at proper times, and I will give you health and peace, and buoyancy of spirits." There is no doubt but your stomachs read you lectures almost daily, on the gratification of your appetites. Do you listen to them, and be instructed? Do you have pains in your stomach, burning sensations, water-brash, flatulency, or rising of wind, an unsatisfied feeling, a craving appetite, sourness, weakness, a bilious tendency, occasional pains and crampings, dyspepsia, or a tendency thereto, heaviness and drowsiness after eating, a tendency to take cold easily, without knowing why, headache, or a heaviness in the brain, a tainted breath, a troubled sleep, wandering or rheumatic pains? Have you one, or any, or all of these? If so, you have a lecture on temperance as often as each one comes. They all tell you that you have been intemperate, that you have indulged some appetite too freely and frequently, that you have transgressed some law, or laws, and ought to return immediately to the simple ways of temperance. They lecture you more to your interests than I can. They give you *home lectures*, "home-thrusts" with the sword of reproof. They announce the fact that ought to startle you, that you are destroying your physical

constitution, and marring the peace and welfare of your mind; and hence are a *sinner*. They are the fore-warnings of death. They tell you you are a self-murderer, that your course is suicidal, that you have already planted a dagger in your own bosom. Why do not these lectures alarm you? Ah, they have been read so slowly and so long in your ears, that you mind them not. Little by little these troubles have come upon you. Slowly down the rippling slope you have glided. You will not believe you are tending toward the pool. But it is so. As surely as there is a pain in your body, so surely you have done wrong.

Pain means penalty, and penalty means that its sufferer should reform. The most of our pains are occasioned by intemperance. This is the fruitful mother of ninety-nine one-hundredths of the diseases that flesh is heir to, and the sins the soul doth commit. We sin by excess of anger, lust, appetite, affection, love of gain, authority, or praise. Few, if any, are the sins that grow not out of intemperance in some form. Intemperance means excess—more of a good thing than is necessary. A thing is good so long as it is necessary. All beyond necessity, or what is necessary, is evil. Money is good; more than what is necessary to the ends of life is evil. Food is good; too much is evil. Light is good; too much will put out our eyes. Water is good; too much will destroy us. Heat is good; too much will burn us. The praise of men is good; too much will ruin us. The love of life is good; too much will make us miserable. Fear is good; too much hath torment. Prayer is good; too much cheats labor of its life, and is evil. Sympathy is good; too much floods us with perpetual grief. Reason is good; too hard pressed with labor, it dethrones the mind and spreads ruin abroad. Any excess in the use or activity of a good thing is intemperance and therefore evil, and to be avoided.

Intemperance, thou mother of harlots, thou abomination of the earth, thou curfew of iniquity, thou breeder of evil, sin, and misery! when will youth learn to abhor thee as they ought, and to spurn thy lascivious allurements with a holy contempt?

But once again, my young friend, when you sit down to your breakfast, and find that the cook has forgotten to prepare the *coffee*, do you feel cross, or sad, or disappointed about it, as though you would have a poor meal, a dry meal, a scant meal, no meal at all, without it? Or, when you come to the supper-table, and find a glass of clear, unadulterated cold water by your plate, and the cook informs you that *she is out of tea*, does the table look bare and dry without it, your appetite fail, your spirits droop, and a chiding, fault-finding spirit rise up within you to complain of something? Or, when you put your hand into your pocket, and find that your *tobacco* is gone, or your *pipe* broken, or your *cigars* smoked up, or your snuff-box empty, do you feel a sort of uneasy, down-in-the-mouth, fish-out-of-water feeling, as though something was wrong, as though your intemperate indulgence had created an appetite which could not now be gratified, as though a morbid, diseased, unnatural condition of some of the organs of your system had been engendered?

These very feelings are temperance lectures. They are voices of warning, presentiments of approaching ruin, of disease and death, which you are bringing upon yourself. They are assurances of the murderous course you are pursuing, cutting daily the threads of life which God has given you to cherish and preserve. The very appetite itself by which these uneasy and unnatural feelings are engendered, is a lecture on temperance, and ought to be so regarded. The very desire for stimulants of any kind, ought to be regarded as a voice of warning against intemperance. This is its true meaning. Says Christ: "He that hateth his brother is a murderer;" "He that lusteth after a woman is an adulterer;" "He that coveteth his neighbor's goods is a thief." He has the murderer, adulterer, and thief in heart. It follows that he that *desires* stimulants, though he may never use them, is intemperate. This unnatural, intemperate desire should be conquered, completely mastered, by a resolute temperance will. We have no right to possess or cherish any such appetites or desires. Evil is in them. And they bid us be wise, and on the look-out. Temperance as a virtue dwells in the heart. It consists in a rigid subjection of every inward feeling and power to the rule of right reason. He who would be thoroughly temperate, must master himself. His passions must be his subjects, obeying his will. From the heart he must be temperate. The youth who would live a temperate life must see to it that the principles of temperance establish their reign in his heart of hearts. He must remember that the intemperance slope is an almost imperceptible one, and that he may be gliding down it when he dreams of naught but safety. He must remember, too, that the field of temperance is a broad one, covering the whole area of life. It is not simply against one form of appetite, one species of indulgence, that he is to guard, but against all The drunkard is not the only intemperate man, nor his the only intemperance we are to fear. It is true, his is a fearful one, a chasm of war, a dark abyss of wretchedness. He is worthy of our deepest commiseration. Charity should flow like a river in his behalf. Pity should become a fountain of tears, and be wept for him. We should make him feel that the souls of the good bleed for him, that all kind people desire and pray for his reform, that the church petitions daily for his return, that there would be joy in a million hearts besides his own, joy on earth, and joy in heaven, if he would reform. All we can feel, and all we can do, we should feel and do for the drunkard. His awful evil we should avoid by touching never one drop of alcoholic poison. It is death, ruin, woe intolerable, horror, living with scorpion stings and remorseless demons. Avoid it! Every youth should detest it, despise it, abhor it with the power of a giant contempt. He should loathe, with sickening disgust, the whole process of drunkard-making. He should spew upon the whole system of liquor-drinking as upon the spawn of hell, which breed naked devils and hot damnation. Frown! He should scowl upon him who asks him to drink, and feel a holy indignation at the dastardly insult.

But while he thus heartily despises the drunkard's intemperance, he should not forget that his is but one form of this giant evil. There are other species of intemperate indulgence of which we are all more or less guilty, even indulgence of appetite, that carries more victims from the earth than does drunkenness, and spreads a wider devastation and a more general blight. We lecture the drunkard day after day and year after year, but seldom think of lecturing ourselves. We have thirty-and-nine lashes for him, and none for ourselves. We have a thousand-and-one good-for-nothing practices, while he has one, just one, of which we complain.

I have often thought that if I was a drunkard, I would lecture back to these good people who talk so loudly of his intemperance, and so little of their own. I would tell them of their teas, and coffees, and tobacco; of their beers, and sodas, and sarsaparillas; of their peppers, spices, and condiments; of their greases, gravies, and indigestible fixings; of their hot rolls, and heavy rolls, and pound rolls; of their tables that groan, and their stomachs that groan worse; of the innocent animals they kill and eat, and of the animals they make of themselves; of the way they live and labor, to eat and live and suffer, after they do eat; of the gouts, rheumatisms, fevers, tumors, cancers, scrofulas, dyspepsias, diarrheas, and thousand-and-one miserable diseases they produce by their miserable intemperance. I should have a wide field to lay open before them, the horrors of which, if they had any hearts, would make them blush—blush to think that they had abased themselves and their neighbors and children so much—not to think they had lectured the drunkard so much, but themselves so little—to think they had transgressed almost as many physical and moral laws as he. If they should tell me of my miserable physical condition, I would read them a lecture on the long list of ailments, pains, and weaknesses which infect their blasted and worn-out bodies, as an offset. Thus, if I were a drunkard, I would be strongly tempted to show those who should attempt to lecture me, that temperance lecturing was a game at which two could play. This, however, would not excuse my drunkenness. It would only be another sad proof that misery loves company. It is evident that if we would induce the drunkard to reform, we must reform ourselves. If we would get the *beam* out of his eye, we must remove the *mote* from our own eye; or else he will say, "Physician, heal thyself," "Preacher, practice thy doctrines." We can not reasonably expect to destroy the use of intoxicating drinks, unless we destroy the many forms of intemperance that lead to the use of such drinks; especially by moral suasion. One kind of intemperance can not well be singled out and rooted alone from the community. This would be unphilosophical in theory, as well as impossible in practice. All kinds of intemperance originate in one plea. They have a common origin—a common parentage. I refer to the various modes of intemperance in the gratification of appetite. One of these can not be singled out and destroyed, while the rest remain in full vigor. The use of strong drinks can not be totally abolished from the community while the use of many other stimulants remain. The reason is obvious. A reformation of this kind must be radical and thorough. It must reach the heart and rest in moral right. It must be a moral reformation, and must be effected by a thorough enlightenment of the moral man.

Such an enlightenment will cure every species of intemperate indulgence of appetite as well as one. A whole community can not be induced to desist from any particular form of indulgence in appetite without being thoroughly enlightened upon the general principles of temperance which cover every form of indulgence. The majority may reform; but I apprehend that it will be exceedingly difficult to work a complete reformation in the whole community, without a general practice of the principles of temperance in all things pertaining to appetite.

All species of intemperance grows out of a want of self-control. To be a temperance man, a man must master himself—must be a brave, noble conquerer of every enemy within his own bosom. It is no small matter. It is the masterpiece of human attainments.

To establish thoroughly and widely the principles of temperance, we must begin with the youth. They have high aspirations to be good and true. They see a glory in the path of right. Freedom is a word of power in their ears. Virtue has many charms, not only for their hearts but for their imaginations. They love health, competency, and happiness. They are ambitious of every good.

When the principles of temperance inculcated in this

lecture are established in early youth, and are made the polar star of life, they will insure health, freedom from pain, competency, respectability, honor, virtue, usefulness, and happiness—yea, all for which true men live or hope in this life. Oh, that they could be general, that all youth would practice them, would build their life edifices upon them! Then would freedom ring out her notes of triumph, religion assert her mild and gentle sway, peace plant her olive wreath in every nation, wisdom, divine and time-honored, shed everywhere her glorious light, and the millennium be established indeed. A race of men and women, full of rosy health, strong, active, symmetrical, beautiful as the artist's model; pure, virtuous, wise, affectionate, full of honor and lofty principle, would grow up into communities and nations, and make the earth bloom and rejoice in more than Eden gladness. A new heaven and a new earth would surround us with beauty, and arch us over with glory, for the old would have passed away.

LECTURE VIII.

AMUSEMENTS.

Laughter is Purely *Human*—Conflicting Opinions on Amusements—Importance of a Right Decision—Amusement a Natural Instinct—Nature a Great and Just Teacher—Why does Man crave Amusement?—Mirthfulness a Primitive Faculty—Hilarity promotes Health—Quality of Amusements—Excess a Source of Dissipation—Exciting Amusements Dangerous—Proper Amusement Spiritual Enjoyment—Amusement should blend with Duty—Home the chief Scene of Amusement—Foreign Amusements Unsafe—Amusement removes Care and Sorrow—Labor and Recreation should not Conflict—Home made Happy by Amusements.

See that man yonder in a fit of laughter. Take a fair look at him; his mouth stretched from ear to ear; his eyes half shut; his whole face in strange contortions; his sides shaking, apparently just ready to burst. A minute more and he may explode. Survey him coolly, with the eye of sober philosophy. Can any thing be more sublimely silly than his appearance? He presents an idea of the ridiculous on a scale of grandeur seldom surpassed. This is the decision of that staid old vinegar-faced philosophy which has had not a little to do in molding human character. Laughing is a *human* amusement, and if not immoderately indulged in, has not a little sound philosophy in it. To laugh just right and at the proper time is practical good sense. Some people exhibit more good sense in laughing than others do in preaching. I have known a laugh express more than a labored essay. Opinions differ about laughing; but my pen is induced to write the con viction, that laughing has a philosophy in it that will not be practically denied for generations to come.

From time immemorial there has been a difference of opinion among men, and women, too, concerning amuse ments. There has been a class of sedate, sober people, who have invariably opposed nearly all amusements which another class of more buoyant and light-hearted natures have felt themselves irresistibly impelled to seek. One has whined, and scolded, and snarled at amusements; the other has plead for them in right good earnest, and some times with a tart sharpness. This difference of opinion has created a war of words, and not unfrequently a war of spirit, which sometimes has been very bitter between the opposing parties. The question has occurred to me, whether there is not really more sin in this warfare than there is in the amusements themselves, admitting them to be as wrong as they are charged with being. Whether it is more sinful to dance, when one does it from very joyous ness of spirit, or to be angry because another has danced, is a question which, it seems to me, is not very difficult to decide, especially in the light of that law which says, "He that is angry with his brother without a cause, is a murderer." Now I would not be understood to believe that this is a question of no importance, but I can not think it worth my while to quarrel with my neighbor about it, for him it is my duty to love. I very much doubt the propriety of quarrelling about any question. I do not think anger is very becoming in any person, not even in a sedate, sober person, much less in a religious one. I once saw a minister half angry. I know "it was not pretty in him." This question of amusements is one that not a little interests the happiness and well-being of society, and is truly worthy of our calm consideration. If I had not deemed the subject worthy of serious attention and thought, I should not have introduced it here, to detain my readers from other interesting and useful subjects. Time is money, and thought is more. Whatever is to affect the time and thoughts of men in this great world is vastly important. That which affects their time and thoughts affects their characters, and their characters affect their moral standing in the sight of God and men, in this world and in the next; and what affects their moral standing affects their peace and happiness. Then this subject is of immense importance, rising in solemn grandeur before us, and inviting the most serious and prayerful consideration. It is more than a question of momentary fun and frolic, but one on the decision of which hang immense and far-reaching consequences. Yea, its results are stupendous. Many a genius of the rarest promise has gone down in a whirlpool of dissipation by a wrong decision of this question. And many a blooming daughter of talent and beauty has become the sport of the most abandoned flatterers, a thing of common contempt, from the same cause. Little do we imagine at first thought the extent and importance of this subject. It affects the whole community. Half the dissipation and wickedness in civilized society grow out of ill-directed

6

amusements; and not a little disease, despondency, and peevishness, originate in a want of proper amusements. Time, money, character, happiness, are all involved in this question. It is a question of philosophy, of political policy and interest, of right and duty, of religion. It is both serious and important. Let us look it in the face. Amusements, it seems to me, are not only right and proper, but absolutely essential to our highest well-being in life. Not only does health require them, but virtue and religion stand in need of them as aids.

In the first place, it may not be amiss to observe that they are *natural.* It seems that the great and beneficent Creator has written in the heart of every living thing the command, "Amuse thyself." And all beings that are *natural*, or that obey the divine laws, written not on parchment but in their very beings, all that yield not to artificial restraints, that have not been cramped in the growth of their powers, have not been manacled by the fetters of an unjust, unnatural, and ungrateful education, yield an agreeable and joyous obedience to this divine command. We are too apt to despise the teachings of nature, as though her voice was not the voice of God; as though she had sinned against the divine behest, and was at war with the Being that made her. If we would learn more of nature and less of the rules of artificial life, far better would it be for us. There is a transcendent beauty in the divine simplicity of nature which we should do well to imitate.

If there is any human being that is more lovely than

any other, it is the one who lives nearest the simplicity of nature, who acts himself as a very child, who personifies his free, unshackled soul in his outward life. When Christ said the kingdom of heaven is composed of little children, He meant that the inhabitants of that free and glorious realm are natural and not artificial, are as God made them, and not as society made them, are subject to the laws written in their own souls, and not to conventional restrictions, are guided implicitly and trustingly by the Spirit of God within them, and not by the spirit of pride and envy aroused by the unholy exactions of a false and sinful state of society. Truly is nature a great and just teacher, and if we can understand her voice we may be confident that it is none other than the voice of the Being Divine. All natural beings are a law unto themselves. And this is the great result aimed at in the gospel. It is to make men natural, a law unto themselves, real children of God.

If, then, we find that amusements are taught by nature, we ought to feel that the instruction is worthy of respect, and be guided by it.

What mean the frolics of the lamb, the gay prances of the horse, the jocund sports of the dog, the gambols of the squirrel amid the tree-tops, the dances of the birds to their own music, on light, fantastic wings? What means the general joy of the animal creation, spoken out in their sports, their endless diversity of amusements, as varied and gay as the colors among flowers, or the forms of beauty on the clouds of heaven? What means the gladsome gayety which rings through the morning air of spring, and gives gladness to the sweet hour of sunset? What means the joyous influence which steals into our own hearts when we go out to make nature a friendly visit, provoking us to sing with the birds and frolic with the lambkins? What means that merry-making inspiration which creeps, in the spirit of mirthfulness, along our every nerve, when we meet with a company of friends who have made glad our hearts with a thousand smiles? What mean the games, plays, feasts, festivals, dances, bonfires, and illuminations which are found in all countries and times, and among all nations of the earth, if they do not declare that amusements are as natural as breath, and as universal as life? What mean the innocent jokes which are flung, in playfulness of spirit, at each other, among all people? What mean the glancing corruscations of wit which glitter in the circles of the best men and women of which our world can boast? What mean all the little pleasantries which pass from tongue to tongue like electric sparks of joy, wherever human beings find pleasure in each other's society? Are they so many evidences of internal depravity? Then, truly, they are beautiful ones, and such as would not mar the peace of heaven. They must be regarded as nature's argument for amusements. Moreover, the instructions of mental science are clear upon this point. That teaches that the Creator of the human mind has written out His will upon this subject, in the faculty of mirthfulness which He has given to every human creature, as a part of its mental character.

We judge that it is right to seek out the relation of

cause and effect in all things, because we are endowed with reason. We believe it right to extend the hand and heart of charity to our fellows, because the principle of benevolence is made a part of our mental constitution, and urges us continually to obey its dictates. We suppose it right to worship God, because we have a mental faculty, the office of which is to worship. We believe it right to be attached to our friends, because we are endowed with an internal power of affection, which will never rest till it is gratified with its desired attainments. So, as we have a mental faculty, the object and office of which is to make and enjoy amusements, and which finds its life-aliment in them, we ought to believe that amusements are right and proper, and are thus established as the legitimate offspring of this mental power which He has conferred upon His creatures.

We thus see that nature with one universal voice teaches amusements; that humanity, speaking out from all nations and times, teaches a lesson on amusements, and that the soul of man, with a voice that can never be mistaken, and should never be unheeded, teaches that it is God's will, written in the mental constitution, that His creature, man, should make himself merry in amusements.

There is much in this world that is dark and gloomy. There are a thousand little troubles, trials, and disappointments, which vex and make us sad. There are hardships, toils, and fatigues, which would wear down and make gloomy our spirits, were it not for this merry-making fellow within us, who spices up life most admirably with his jocularity and sport. Nothing is more paralyzing to the mental energies, or more destructive of moral power, than a fixed and sullen sadness, or a cold, cheerless, benighted state of mind.

Cheerfulness is absolutely essential to the mind's healthy action, or the performance of its proper duties. The mind unmoved by the spirit which dwells in amusements, unvisited by the gales of mirthfulness, is like the ocean sleeping in the cold lap of earth, unmoved by a breeze and unstirred by a tide. It is still, pulseless, powerless, and will soon become stagnant, dead—a great pool of corruption, in which no living thing can dwell, from which no healthful influence can go out. Without the influence of this same spirit of cheerfulness, the body would lose its vitality, would grow cold, inert, feeble, sickly; making not only a cheerless and lonely dwelling-place for the mind, but one sickly and miasmatic. No charming habitation, no sweet, healthy home, no sunny elysium, where all its faculties and powers can bathe themselves in light, and breathe the fresh, wholesome airs of young life, can it find in such a body. Nothing gives more of real vitality of body, sparkling in the rosy cheek, and elastic step, and symmetrical beauty, than a due amount of proper and well-directed amusement. And, as a healthy and uncontaminated body is necessary for a pure and elevated mind, it follows that the intellectual, moral, and social condition of the being within is improved by the vigor and glow of health given by the cheerful influences of amusements. But the question more difficult to decide to the satisfaction of all is, as to what amusements are proper, what gives the glow of health to the physical and moral man, and impair not in any manner the rightful and proper action of either. Some amusements are good and some bad. In nothing is sound judgment more needed than in the choice of amusements. It does not follow that because amusements are proper and useful, every thing is proper that is amusing. Very much of the good of amusements depends upon the *kind*, and still more the *amount*.

I. And this leads me to remark that amusements, whatever they may be, should not be *immoderately exciting*.

There is always a tendency in the human mind to go to some extreme, to the end of the road it is traveling. Give it rope enough and it will hang itself. It is so in labor, in rest, in politics, religion, and all things; and especially so in amusements. As a general thing, that faculty which is gratified most pleads the most for more. Extremes in amusements, like extremes in every thing else, are injurious. Whenever they are made unduly exciting, or are carried to excess, they become absolutely evil. They dissipate the mind, intoxicate the brain with the wild enthusiasm of delight, waste the solid energies of the soul, destroy the equilibrium of the faculties, break up their harmonious action, and establish a positive discord within; besides being injurious to the health. To be drunk with amusement is more injurious than to be drunk with alcohol. It is a paralysis of all lofty purposes and moral vigor. A trifling, good-for-nothing thing is a soul intoxicated with amusements.

It is the evil of this excess in amusements that has stamped them with a stigma in the minds of many of the more sober and sedate. They have seen the evil, and deplored it. There is a greater tendency to abuse amuse ments than almost any thing else, on account of their exhilarating effects. They produce a sort of intoxication in the animal spirits, which imparts itself to the mind, and leads it on in a bewilderment of superabundant life, not un frequently to an injurious excess. Among real lovers of amusements they are almost always abused. They are permitted to occupy too much attention, and the giddy maze of their follies becomes a whirl of dissipation. There is great danger of this among active, buoyant, high spirited youth. Those of such a nature should be ex tremely cautious in the kind of amusements they choose, avoiding the most exciting, and in the influence they per mit them to have upon their minds. There is great dan ger in excesses. They should be avoided always. The most scrupulous watchfulness should be entertained by every such youth against these excesses. The gay dream of merriment should never become bewildering, should never unfit us for the performance of our duties, should never make cheerless and uninviting the solid avocations of life.

The first step in excess is one step in sin. We must always remember that the kingdom of evil borders closely upon the kingdom of good. Wrong is the next-door neighbor to right. Intemperance is only one step from emperance Sin begins where righteousness ends. Disobedience joins possessions with obedience. This should teach us to keep discretion on the watch-tower with vigil ance by his side, that we may never become intoxicated with gayety, nor rudely excited with amusement. This is the rock on which many a youth has split his bark of life. Amusements have dissipated his mind, stolen his heart, corrupted his manners and morals, eaten up his earnings, made him the child of folly, and the dupe of an insatiable desire for a life of giddiness. The soundest wisdom should not only direct our amusements but our enjoyment of them. The more exciting any amusement is, the more dangerous it is. I say *dangerous*, yes, *dangerous*—that is the word. It is truly so.

Alluring are the paths of folly, that lead out in many directions from the scenes of intoxicating amusements. Amuse yourself in moderation, youth. Be not intemperate. All the good of any amusement comes from its use in moderation. The object of amusements is not to intoxicate, but to make cheerful; not to bewilder, but to enlighten; not to degrade, but to elevate. Be prudent, be cautious, be wise. Be glad, but not rude. Be happy, but not wild. Be gay, but not boisterous. Be simple, but not silly.

II. People usually seek amusements, as they say, "for the fun of it." They seek them to "kill time," to dissipate sorrow, for their stimulating effects, etc. They have no high purpose in view, and hence get no elevated good from them. To have their proper influence, amusements must be sought, not simply "to have a good time," but for their healthy and invigorating influence upon the body and mind. We should seek them for their real utility. We should enjoy them because we feel that they are right; because they are of real service to moral and accountable beings; because they increase our capacities for real enjoyment; because they harmonize our powers, quicken our activities, accelerate the pulses of both the inner and outer life, humanize our feelings, and refine our sympathies. We should seek them as we would any other good, as we would a feast of reason or flow of soul, as a duty which we owe ourselves and the world. This gives them a moral aspect, places them among the means of moral improvement. Then the moral feelings enjoy them, the conscience enters into the gladness, the whole upper soul sparkles with delight. Most thrillingly intense is the pleasure of amusements thus rationally enjoyed. They are not then merely animal pleasures, but spiritual enjoyments. They should really stand side by side with the institutions of morality and religion, as aids, and not enemies to these. There are many excellent and useful amusements which have become degrading in the eyes of many good people, from their abuse. They have done real evil, have sown the seeds of vice, and brought forth rich harvests of woe. They have been prostituted to evil, till they are now altogether corrupt in their influences. They might be mighty engines for moral good, whereas they are instruments of untold corruption. They have not been sought and enjoyed with a proper view, and have been abused on this account. This abuse has very naturally brought reproach upon the amusements themselves.

If we would regard amusements as a part of our education, a part of the moral training which we must receive to perfect our natures and refine our sympathies, very differently would they be viewed. Much, very much, might well-conducted and well-chosen amusements do to render us more interesting and agreeable to each other, more graceful, free, and natural in our manners, and more ready and able to perform well our various duties in life. Much more cheerful, refined, kind, and happy, might society be made by the influence of proper amusements, sought with a view to refine, elevate, and gladden the whole moral and physical being.

III. To be really useful, amusements should be intimately blended with all the labors of life. Instead of being entirely separated from every thing else, and set apart by themselves at some chosen place and time, they should mingle with, and color with a ray of brightness, the whole web of life. They should be made so easy of access, so much at hand, and so readily attained, that without much effort, or expense, or loss of time, they might gladden life with their sunshine, give vermilion to the blood, and a joy to the soul upward every day. When they are sought only at certain seasons of festivity, at long intervals of time, and then with great pomp and eclat, they are almost sure to be abused. They generally result in absolute evil. They become scenes of improper excitement, and not unfrequently of trouble and discord. They engage too much the thoughts, fix too strongly the attention, they bewilder and dazzle too much the mind. And when they are over, no good can be determined upon with any degree of certainty, and often much evil is clearly the result. Such amusements are unnatural and improper, and should be everywhere discouraged. To be profitable, amusements should be frequent and simple, such as give grace and vigor to the body, animation and vivacity to the mind, refinement to the manners, and harmony and happiness to the whole being. To do this, they must be skillfully and frequently interspersed with the business, and duties, and ordinary avocations of life. They should give cheerfulness, vivacity, and peace, to every-day life. And in seasons when they can, they should be sought out of doors, in the open, health-giving air, among the bright, gay things of nature; on the hills, amid the vales; in the groves; by the sparkling cascade; where there is life and beauty; where every thing has a voice of instruction and a song of joy. And they should be made, so far as possible, intellectually and morally interesting. They should be mingled with our studies, interspersed with our labors, and woven into the web of life; but should always be directed by judgment and sanctioned by virtue, propriety, and rectitude.

IV. It is a clear dictate of reason, that the chief scene of amusements should be at home. Around home clusters all that the heart holds dear. Here is the scene of the most of our labors and trials. Here are our chief joys, our bitterest sorrows. Here are nearly all our real experiences in life. Here are our wants, and here should be our supplies, and here should be the scene of our gayety, merriment, and joy. Here should be the real music of life. Here should be its gladdest pleasures, its mirth and sprightliness. There is but little danger from an excess of home amusements. Dissipation is usually found abroad. Injurious excitements are nearly all away from home. The evils of amusements are absent from this sacred place. At home amusements may be guarded from all harm. Associates and associations may be such as they should be. Amusements may here be varied at pleasure and directed at will. One reason why amusements have become objects of dread with many people is, because they have been driven from the sacred protection of the fireside; they have been exiled from the only place where they can be safely indulged in, and banished to places from which, in truth, modesty and virtue ought to shrink back. They have been forced amid associations corrupt and evil. Having been found in bad company, they have been dishonored. If they had been kept at home, where they should be, they might still have been honored guests of that blessed sanctuary. Thousands of youth have been ruined or greatly injured, in a moral point of view, by feeling compelled to go away from home for the amusements which their natures impelled them to desire.

Every home should be a little world, furnishing at least a little of all that its inmates want to make them happy. Let parents see well to this, and they will not be compelled to see their children weary of home. I do feel that our homes are not what they should be; they are not attractive enough; are not furnished with such places and means of sport, play, feats, tricks, as the wants of children and youth require. Every home should have a play-ground and play-room, with the means to practice all the little innocent sports that childhood and youth are so ready to invent and engage in. There should be a season set apart every day, when it is practicable, when some kind of amusement should be engaged in. It may be simply conversation brisk and active, or it may be a regular child-like frolic; any thing to unbend both body and mind. There is more *rest* often in an hour's amusement than in a whole night's repose. Rest, either of body or mind, is found in change, more than repose. The care-ladened mind recovers quickly from its fatigue, when its cares are thrown off in some jocund sport or scene of wit. The wearied body will often recruit its activity and strength with brisk bodily exercise, in some stirring and interesting amusement. How often does the sober old grand-dame fretfully exclaim to the troop of children and youth about her, "Never too tired to play." How many thousand times have I heard that rung in the ears of happy young people, who were enjoying a scene of merriment, after a hard day's labor, as though they were absolutely wasting strength. The truth is, they were gaining strength. It is no expenditure of strength or energy to enjoy heartily a proper amusement, when one is fatigued. Youth should never be too tired to engage in either physical or mental amusement. When they are thus fatigued their bodies are over-taxed.

It is wicked thus to wear out young life, and health, and strength. All young people should labor, and labor briskly; and so should children. They should always have their daily labors, in which they may make themselves useful. No duty is more binding than this; and no philosophy more plain than that which points out this. But that labor should never be so hard as to crush their spirits, or so fatigue their bodies that they have no relish for amusements. Often in early youth have I come from the field of labor at night, after working briskly and cheerfully all day, and thrown a ball against the barn for a full hour, all alone, just because I loved to do it; or jumped on a pole, over all the fences about the homestead; or run for an hour on the tops of stone walls and board fences, to try my skill at balancing; and then retired to rest, refreshed by my sports. I know, by a happy experience, that labor only makes amusements all the more agreeable and useful. Give me the youth that labor, for real sport. They understand the "fun of it." Amusements, like rest, can not be enjoyed without previous labor. Then again, frequently have I come from the field, so jaded and weary that every muscle in my body moaned for rest, when amusements looked disgusting, and the door-stone was a soft bed; where for an hour I would lie in refreshing stupor, before retiring. That was labor with a vengeance. But the fault was mine. Young ambition prompted it. Such labor I know to be injurious.

Bitter experience has taught me, that when youth are too fatigued to enjoy amusements, they have over-worked.

A proper amount of labor, well-spiced with sunny sports, is almost absolutely necessary to the formation of a firm, hardy, physical constitution, and a cheerful and happy mind. Let all youth not only learn to choose and enjoy proper amusements, but let them learn to invent them at home, and use them there, and thus form ideas of such homes as they shall wish to have their own children enjoy. Not half the people know how to make a home. It is one of the greatest and most useful studies of life to learn how to make a home—such a home as men, and women, and children should dwell in. It is a study that should be early introduced to the attention of youth. It would be well if books were written upon this most interesting subject, giving many practical rules and hints, with a long chapter on *Amusements*

LECTURE IX.

MUSIC.

What Music really is—Power and Influence of Music—The Soul Baptized in Music—Music a Universal Language—The Harmony of the Universe—Music is the Voice of Love—Music the Voice of Worship—Cultivation of Music—Music a Spiritualizer—Prostitution of Music—Music an Essential of Education.

MUSIC is the poetry of sound. It embraces harmony, concord, and melody. It moves with the succession of the same or similar sounds, and moves on velvet wings, waved so gently and gracefully, that naught but onward motion is known or felt. Whatever sound produces the charm of melody in the soul, wakes up all its Eolian strings to breathing symphonies within, unheard, but felt like the spirit-notes of a rapt vision, is music. Whatever sound, or succession of sounds, makes us forget that we are dwellers of earth, and lifts us, for the time being, into a world of living harmonies, which come and go, entrance and bewilder, captivate and hold in trembling delight our minds, like the electric color-dances of the Aurora Borealis, is real music. It is a thing to be *felt*, not *described*. It is not sound simply; for all sound is not music. It is a peculiar, indescribable running together, or blending of certain smooth sounds of different heights, like the gliding together of the different colors of the rainbow. Its presence is tested only by the charm wrought in the soul.

When the soul is in ecstasy, occasioned by a succession of sounds, we may know that music numbers are flowing. When a soft sound starts a tear in the eye, we may know that the spirit of music is there. O the rapturous charm of Music! What power it has to soften, melt, enchain in its spirit-chords of subduing harmony! Truly there is power in music; an almost omnipotent power. It will tyrannize over the soul. It will force it to bow down and worship, it will wring adoration from it, and compel the heart to yield its treasures of love. Every emotion, from the most reverent devotion to the wildest gushes of frolicsome joy, it holds subject to its imperative will. It calls the religious devotee to worship, the patriot to his country's altar, the philanthropist to his generous work, the freeman to the temple of liberty, the friend to the altar of friendship, the lover to the side of his beloved. It elevates, empowers, and strengthens them all. The human soul is a mighty harp, and all its strings vibrate to the gush of music. Yet all souls are not the same harp, nor are all affected alike by its power. Some will listen to the most exquisite music with only an agreeable pleasure, while others are carried heavenward in a whirlwind of bewildering joy.

One writer describes the effect of Lizst's piano, playing upon him, in the following enthusiastic strain: "With blow after blow upon the instrument, with his whole force, he planted large columnar masses of sound, like the Giant's Causeway. The instrument rained, hailed, thundered, moaned, whistled, shrieked, round those basaltic columns in every cry that the tempest can utter in its wildest par oxysms of wrath." . . . . . "Then we were borne along through countless beauties of rock, and sky, and foliage, to a grotto, by the side of which was a fountain, that seemed one of the eyes of the earth, so large and darkly brilliant was it, so deep and so serene. Here we listened to the voices rather than the songs of birds, when the music by degrees diminished, then fluttered and ceased."

Mrs. Childs speaks thus of her sensations at listening to the music of a master of this divine art: "How he did it, I know as little as I know how the sun shines or how the spring brings forth its blossoms. I only know that music came from his soul into mine, and carried it upward to worship with angels." . . . . . "It overcame me like a miracle. I felt that my soul was for the first time baptized in music; that my spiritual relations were somehow changed by it, and that I should henceforth be otherwise than I had been. I was so oppressed with 'the exceeding weight of glory,' that I drew my breath with difficulty. As I came out of the building, the street sounds hurt me with their harshness. The sight of ragged boys and unfortunate coachmen jarred more than ever on my feelings. I wanted that the angels that had ministered to my spirit, should attend theirs also. It seemed to me that such music should bring all the world into the harmonious beauty of divine order. I passed by my earthly home, and knew it not. My spirit seemed to be floating through infinite space. The next dav I felt like a person who had been in a trance, seen heaven opened, and then returned to earth again."

Says another writer of a great musician: "His soul is but a harp, which an infinite breath modulates; his senses are but strings, which weave the passing air into rythm and cadence." Wonderful, indeed, is the power of music; and all are more or less the subjects of its mysterious charms. And this leads me to remark, that music is *universal.*

Different nations have different habits, customs, manners, modes of expression, and different words and languages to convey their thoughts and feelings. But music is felt alike by them all. A stirring strain will touch the well-strung souls of every nation alike. All will dance to a note of joy; all will weep to one of sadness. A lofty strain will bear all to heaven, a jarring discord sink them back to earth. The same masters have made the same music in Norway, Germany, Italy, France, England, America, and all have bowed before it like reeds before the blast. A beautiful proof is this of the kindred nature of all souls, of the existence of a mysterious link of spiritual union, that binds them all together. And the beauty of this proof is hightened when we remember that music is the *voice* of *love*, and is closely allied to the infinite. Love speaks in tones of music. Love breaths musical airs. Love delights to pour itself out in song. The lover of God chants his praises in strains of lofty music. Witness the sweet singer of Israel, the prophets, the songs of angels, the aspirations breathed in music of every devout soul. The lover of freedom speaks his love in song.

The lover of beauty sings its praises. The lover of humanity softly breathes his love-notes in strains of sweetest music. Then how beautiful is its universality! The *love* of which it is the voice is equally universal. All souls have *love* within them. Love, or Good, is the inmost essence of all things. It is the all-pervading soul of the universe. Its *voice* is music. It is breathed in the harmony of the spheres, in the anthem of universal nature. The winds, the seas, the lightnings, the forests, the mountains, the beasts, the birds, the insects, the little brooks, and, most of all, the noblest work of God on earth, give utterance to its voice, the voice of love, the music of creation. I have fancied sometimes that I could perceive the great Being of Love sitting in the mid-heavens, clothed in light, with the rainbow-arch above His throne, listening with infinite pleasure to the anthem of creation in its infinite swells and falls, catching the silver notes of the least little organist, and delighting His ear with the full chorus of boundless harmony which His own diffusive love had raised throughout the infinitude of His works.

It has been beautifully said that, "Music is the voice of God, and poetry His language." God's love is infinite, and so, in its highest achievements, music expresses to us much of the infinite. It seems to bear an affinity to God. Says Mrs. Childs, of the impression made on her mind by a musical performance: "It expressed to me more of the *infinite* than I ever saw, or heard, or dreamed of, in the realms of nature, art, or imagination." And again she says: "Music is the soprano, the feminine principle, the heart of the universe. Because it is the voice of Love, because it is the highest type, and aggregate expression of passional attraction, therefore it is infinite; therefore it pervades all space, and transcends all being, like a divine influx. What the tone is to the word, what expression is to the form, what affection is to thought, what the heart is to the head, what intuition is to argument, what insight is to policy, what religion is to philosophy, what holiness is to heroism, what moral influence is to power, what woman is to man, is music to the universe. Flexile, graceful, and free, it pervades all things, and is limited by none. It is not poetry, but it is the *soul* of poetry; it is not mathematics, but it is *in* numbers, like harmonious proportions in cast iron; it is not in painting, but it shines through colors, and gives them their tone; . . it is not in architecture, but the stones take their places in harmony with its voice, and stand in 'petrified music.'" In the words of Bettina: "Every art is the body of music, which is the soul of every art; and so is music to the soul of love, which also answers not for its workings; for it is the contact of divine with human."

Besides music being powerful, universal, the voice of love, and the type of the infinite, it is *venerable* for its *age*. As it is the voice of God's love, we know not but it is coexistent with His being. It is reasonable to suppose that its swelling numbers have rolled and made heaven vocal with its strains of praise since creation dawned. But the first account of it on record was at the laying of the foundations of the earth, when the "morning stars" delighted with the promise of a new planet, "sang together, and all the sons of God shouted for joy." As soon as the earth was made, its rocky spires thrown up, its forest harps strung, its ocean organs tuned, it raised its everlasting anthem to swell the chorus of the skies.

All God's devout children of the human kind have raised songs of praise to their Maker. His men inspired have loved to dedicate their powers, to string the harp and tune the psalter to the voice of sacred song. Music being the voice of God and being universal, we see that nature invites, in the language of inspiration: "Come, let us sing unto the Lord." Music being the voice of love, how appropriate a vehicle is it to bear up to the great home of everlasting love the incense of human affections. Sing unto the Lord, because He is Love. Sing to Him, because music is the voice of love. Sing to Him, because He loves the songs of devout hearts. Sing unto Him, because a sacred song melts the heart in love to Him. Sing unto Him, because music elevates the soul to heaven. Sing to Him, because music is the type of the infinite, and enlarges the sphere of our thoughts and aspirations. Sing unto Him, because music is the link unseen that binds all hearts in one, and all with God. Sing unto Him, because singing is the employment of angels, and will be ours when angel crowns we wear. Come, let us sing unto the Lord, is the voice of reason, of love, of revelation, and nature. Let us sing now, and make earth vocal with His praises; sing while in this life, that we may be the better prepared when we go hence, to sing—

"That undisturbed song of pure consent,
Aye sung around the sapphire-colored throne,
To Him that sits thereon:
* * * * * * * *
Where the bright seraphim in burning row
Their loud uplifted angel trumpets blow;
And the cherubic hosts, in thousand choirs,
Touch their celestial harps of golden wires."

The human voice is the most perfect musical instrument ever made; and well it might be, for it had the most skillful Maker. That voice should be cultivated to sing the tones of love to man and to God. Around the fireside, in the social circle, it should sing the voice of love, and at the altar of God it should pour forth melodious praise.

Who does not know the softening power of music, especially the music of the human voice? It is like the angel-whisperings of kind words in the hour of trouble. Who can be angry when the voice of love speaks in song? Who hears the harsh voice of selfishness, and brutalizing passion, when music gathers up her pearly love-notes, to salute the ear with a stray song of paradise? Sing to the wicked man, sing to the disconsolate, sing to the sufferer, sing to the old, and sing to children, for music will inspire them all.

To all youth we would say, cultivate well the powers of music in your souls, for amply will you be repaid. God has given you the talent for music; shall it be useless within you for want of use? Shall the gem never be burnished? Shall you never present it shining to God, its giver, in a song of praise and worship. It is due to Him that it should be cultivated. It should be taught to breathe the soul-stirring harmonies of the sanctuary in the ear of Almighty Love. How sweet does it make the worship of God, to have the reverent emotions poured out in song! How early should children be taught to sing; for what is sweeter than the songs of innocent childhood, so refining, so refreshing, so suggestive of heaven? Music sweetens the cup of bitterness, softens the hand of want, lightens the burdens of life, makes the heart courageous, and the soul cheerfully devout. Into the soul of childhood and youth it pours a tide of redeeming influence. Its first and direct effect is to mentalize the musical performer; not to give him knowledge, nor more wisdom in the practical, business affairs of life, but to stir his mental being to activity, to awaken strong emotions, to move among the powers within as a common electrifier, touching here with tenderness, there with energy, now with holy aspiration, and anon with the inspiring thrill of beauty. It breathes like a miracle of inspiration through the soul, to elevate, refine, and spiritualize. No lethargy can exist in the soul that is pouring forth a tide of music numbers. Its very recesses are all astir. Every thing within becomes active; the perceptions acute, the affections warm, the moral sensibilities quick and sensitive. When we think how much the world wants awakening, we can think of no power better calculated to do it than that which dwells in the mysterious melodies of music. Let every body become musicians, and surely they would become *living* souls. The *dead* would be raised;

the stupid vitalized, and the enervate, mindless creature of *ennui* stirred into a breathing, active, emotional existence.

But it not only gives an additional warmth, fervor, and vigor to the powers within; it gives refinement. It is opposed to the gross, the low, and the vulgar. Music never suggests vulgarity and baseness, never tends to the coarse and low. To the shame of humanity be it said, that it has been prostituted to administer to passions base and feelings vile. And so has religion, and reason, and love. But not more are these directly opposed to the vile and coarse than is music. When music numbers take hold of the mental man with their powerful and vigorous sway, and raise it to that point of activity and emotional fervor scarcely ever attained by any other means, the whole tendency is to the pure, the refined, and the perfect. It is true the increased and cultivated sensibility of musical performers makes them so alive to discord, opposition, harshness, that at times they become much like that sensitive plant called "touch-me-not," but this is rather the result of outward inharmony than of inward tendency to irritability. The outward world is not in harmony with their inward world. It is too gross and rough, too discordant and perplexing.

It must be expected that the sensibility which music cultivates will extend to the passional as well as the moral nature of man; and will at times make anger more acute as well as love. It gives an increased activity to the whole being. And this would show the importance of cultivating all the mental powers in harmony with the musical talent. Much as I prize the influences of music, holy and enrapturing as I believe them to be, I would not press its claims beyond its proper limits. Harmony of mental development should be the grand object of life. The real and all-glorious influences of music are known and felt only when the whole mind is truly and properly cultivated. Then its charm is perfect; then its heaven is created. Music should be an essential part of education. It should be cultivated with numbers, with science, with literature, and poetry; for it is intimately blended with all these, is the spiritual expression of them all. It should begin ere words are lisped by the infant tongue, and be continued through the whole educational course, yea, through life. On account of its mentalizing tendency, it assists rather than retards the educational progress. It renders more active all the mental powers; so that the whole educational work is assisted by the vitalizing power of the musical faculties. An education can be acquired quicker and more effectually with, than without, the cultivation of the musical talent. The time given to that augments as rapidly as time spent in any other way the strength of the mental powers, while it relaxes, unbends, and thus rests and strengthens them, thus giving more time to the real work of education. Then let all youth be wise, and educate their talents for heavenly music.

LECTURE X.

CHASTITY OF LANGUAGE.

A word fitly spoken is like apples of gold in pictures of silver."—*Proverbs.*

Mind, the fountain of Happiness and Misery—Creation, the Embodied Thought of God—Power and Dignity of Language—Charm of Pure Language—Groveling Minds employ Vulgar Words—Home, the place for Pure Speech—Home, the School of Life—Simplicity, the Beauty of Speech—By-words Vulgar—By-words Senseless—Profane Swearing—Evils of Profanity—Quaker Anecdote—Pure Dress of Thought.

I INTRODUCE to the attention of my young friends in this lecture a subject which I deem of much importance, not only to their own happiness and well-being, but to their usefulness in the world. It is *Chastity of Language.* Some may think, at the first view, that this is hardly worthy of a whole lecture. But if not, what is worthy of careful instruction? Language is the vehicle of thought and feeling. Thought and feeling are the spontaneous expressions of the states of the mind. The state of the mind is the fountain of both happiness and misery. Thus, it is of great importance that the vehicle of the product of mind be chaste and pure, that the influence thus borne from mind to mind may be of the best possible kind.

Remember, language is the vehicle of the product of mind, that immortal essence which produces thought, that godlike principle of being which formed the rolling spheres, balanced the dancing universe, and filled immensity with the splendid garniture of the skies. It is the vehicle of that even which is of itself immortal. For who can say that thought is not as imperishable as that which produces it? What is the earth on which we dwell but a thought of God? What are those eternal laws upon which rest all the order, magnificence, and reality of the heavens and the earth, but the thoughts of God? What are the stars that glitter above us; what are the suns that warm and illumine the boundless field of ethereal glory; what are the bright intelligences that wing day and night the glorious airs of the celestial world; what are human creatures; what are minds in earth, but the thoughts of God? What is the universe in all its gorgeous grandeur, in all its star-built and sun-proved glory, but one great, magnificent, eternal thought of God? All this great assemblage of the products of the Eternal Mind, is the burden of human language. So the mightiest thoughts that have grown up in the creature's mind are the burden of language. All that the Homers, Miltons, Newtons, Addisons, Howards, and Channings of earth have thought, or felt, or seen, or known, has been given to human language to bear to kindred minds down through the rush of coming ages. Even the rich treasures of Heavenly wisdom, the oracles of Divine love, have been intrusted to the keeping of this same carrier of all sacred things. An instrument thus important, thus glorious in its uses, thus grand in the results of its employment, surely is not unworthy of our attention, not unworthy of our study. If it has been and still is employed to convey the lively images that come into being within us from soul to soul, and thus form a link between intelligences, a telegrapher of the internal states, it is surely second only, as a subject of interest and study, to the thoughts or states of mind which it conveys.

The capabilities and powers of the language which we speak are singularly great and wonderful. It is so flexible and yielding, so ready and susceptible, that it will take upon itself all the varieties of thought, and modes of feel ing, all the million states of mind and heart which are found in the existence of the human soul, and convey them to others with the utmost ease and simplicity of expression. It is true, it can not scale the highest hills of thought, nor sound the lowest depths of feeling. It can not tell the heart's deepest griefs nor most ecstatic joy, nor the mind's most exquisite conceptions of beauty or excellency. But sufficient is it for all the ordinary uses of humanity. It will convey our warm impulses of tenderness and love, our earnest sympathies for the sick and sorrowing, our glowing thoughts, and the live embers of our philanthropy. It will fill our minds with the radiant light, and our hearts with the sparkling joy of others. It will open to us treasuries of wisdom, which are around us, and which have accumulated in immense profusion, during the slow lapse of centuries in which it has been employed to chronicle the thoughts and deeds of men. It will bring around us the great and the good of all past ages for our friends and companions, and familiarize us with what they saw, and, heard, and thought, and felt; and will inform us of the world as it is. Comprehending, then, the importance of the uses of language, we can not fail to see the importance of making it a perpetual study, especially when we remember that it bears the same relation to ideas that beauty does to virtue, as expressed by an excellent writer: "Beauty makes virtue appear more lovely still." So, chaste, refined, and appropriate language adds a new charm, even to the most beautiful thought. Ordinary thoughts, and the common conceptions of mankind, when clothed in the comely garb of pure, refined, and flowing words, become to us truly delightful, and awaken the sweet and tender sensibilities of our better natures. The conversation of a person of only common abilities and attainments is deeply pleasing, and often thrillingly interesting, when words joined in harmonious relations and expressive of real refinement and sensibility, are chosen as the symbols of thought and emotion. "Words fitly spoken are like apples of gold in pictures of silver." Charmingly delightful are they to the ear of a soul of refined and tender sensibilities. They fall upon it like notes of music, and thrill and tremble there in cadences which bring the soul into harmony with all beautiful things.

We are always delighted with well-chosen and appropriate language in a public address. The orator's power lies much in the stirring music-notes of the language he employs. He rings a thousand changes in words. If refined and elegant language is delightful in a public speaker, how much more so is it in private conversation, in the social circle, in the converse of friend with friend, of lover with lover, of companion with companion? It is in the private walks of life that the deepest, and strongest, and loveliest feelings of our natures are called into action. The relations of kindred, friends, and companions, in which are opened the heart's fountains of love and goodness, are in their most delightful aspects and offices concealed from the world. They are too tender and sweet to bear the gaze of a rude world. Here is it that the power, beauty and refinement of human language should be chiefly known and felt. Here it is that it should become the music-notes of the most refined affection. Here it is that the euphony of its flute-like power should thrill along the nerves of those whom love has united in its harp-strings' bonds.

The home circle should be held too sacred to be polluted with the vulgarities of language which could have origin ated nowhere but in low and groveling minds. It should be dedicated to love and truth, to all that is tender in feel ing and noble and pure in thought, to the holiest com munions of soul with kindred soul. In order that such a communion may be fully enjoyed, it is requisite that lan guage should there perform its most sacred office, even the office of transmitting unimpaired the most tender and sacred affections that glow in the human heart.

Home! how sweet, how tender the word! How full of the associations that the heart loves! How deeply inter-woven are the golden filaments of these associations with all the fibers of our affectionate natures, forming the glit-tering web of the heart's golden life! Here are father, mother, child, brother, sister, companions, all the heart loves—all that makes earth lovely, all that enriches the mind with faith and the soul with hope! What language is meet for home use, to bear the messages of home feelings, to be freighted with the diamond-treasures of home hearts? Should it be any other than the most refined and pure—any other than that breathing the sacred chastity of affection?

If the dialect of angels could be used on earth, its fittest place would be in the home circle. The dialect of home should be such as would not stain an angel's tongue, nor fall harshly on an angel's ear. It should be made up of the words of wisdom, which are at once the glory of youth and the honor of age. If the members of every home would use that language, and that only which the true home-feeling inspires, and which should be used in filling the true offices of that only earthly prototype of heaven, how different would be the appearance of the world. Methinks we should then have no need of angel visitors to teach us the ways of love and joy, of peace and glory; for earth would have its own angels, and they would be scarcely inferior to those that dwell above. The language that would fall from their tongues would be indeed like "apples of gold in pictures of silver," and its influence upon other hearts would be like the breathings of angel melodies. Home is not only the proper place for the *use* of pure and refined language, but it is the place to learn that language which we wish to use abroad—that language which we would speak in the most refined circles of society, which becomes the pure heart and chaste tongue. If we would speak an undefiled language away from home, in the presence of the good, the pure, the learned, we must speak it at home. Home is the place where we form many, if not the most of our habits, both of action and speech. These habits we carry into the world. They cling to us like leeches. The vulgarities which we use at home we shall use abroad. The coarse sayings, the low jests, the vulgar phrases, the grammatical blunders, all the lingual improprieties which go to form a part of our home conversation, will enter into our conversation at all times and in all places. If we permit vile bar-room sayings, street rigmaroles, and clownish vulgarisms, to stain our tongues at home, we shall be sure to have them blistered with these same idle, worse than idle things, in places where we shall be mortified to hear them fall from our own lips. How often in refined company have I seen the blush of shame tinge the cheeks of persons who at home, parrot-like, catch up all the vulgarisms that come out like vomit from the mouths of the polluted. Be assured, my young friends, that your language at home will give character and tone to your language abroad, and that your language in the most refined circles in which you may mingle will tell a sure tale of your home language. There is but one way to have a pure and chaste speech: that is, to cultivate at home the common use of those words which are like apples of gold in pictures of silver. To be successful in this, you must first cultivate pure and refined thoughts and feelings, and then give the freest, easiest, and most agreeable expression to them that your knowledge of words will permit. Strive always for the most pleasing and musical forms of expressions; those which are clear, unambiguous, having no double meaning, and at the same time so appropriate and chaste that they would sound equally well in the refined drawing-room, the public lecture hall, or from the sacred desk. In doing this, you need not seek pompous words, great swelling phrases. These, as a general rule, are gross vulgarisms, as offensive to a refined taste as many of a coarser yet simpler nature. What you want is a child-like simplicity of speech, united with a purity of word and diction which can not offend the ears of the most ardent lovers of literary refinement. Think not that I recommend any stiffness of speech, or a long, round set of phrases, which come and go like the tide, by an eternal law; or that soft, silly, simpering affectedness, which is so strangely precise that each word must be pinched out, by rule, between the tongue and the lips. These are forms of vulgarity as truly detestable as any other. I would have language come from the tongue as easily and as purely as a song from the throat of a bird; and have such language always chosen as shall dress in the most becoming manner the idea to be delivered. To secure this most desirable end, language must be our study, our practical every-day study. We should learn, by perpetual practice, to clothe our common ideas in a simple, easy dress, a purely chaste expression, and clothe them with a gracefulness of manner and an elegance of diction, which is proper for all places. Thus will our *words be like apples of gold in pictures of silver.* Some sound writer has said, that greatness consists not so much in doing *extraordinary actions* as in doing *common actions* in an extraordinary *manner.* So the beauty and power of language is not shown so much in clothing *extraordinary ideas* as in clothing *common thoughts* in an *extraordinary manner.* It is common thoughts with which we have the most to do, and these we should seek to express in the most appropriate and becoming manner.

There are two particulars connected with this general subject, to which I wish to call especial attention. And I would that all could be so impressed with correct views upon these points that they shall never again be guilty of the errors to which I refer. The first is "*by-words.*" Nothing is more common, especially among the young, than a frequent use of by-words. The habit is so confirmed with many young persons, that they can hardly speak a single sentence without interlarding it with some vulgar by-word, or some low, detestable Billingsgate saying, which is altogether destitute both of wit and sense. There are a thousand-and-one of these common by-words in frequent use, by those who really fancy they are quite refined in their language. Almost any *lady*, even, thinks she has a perfect right to inflict upon every body's ears a score or two of "*law-me's,*" "*my gracious's,*" and "*mercy on me's!*" in a conversation of ten minutes, upon any subject. How many of these common-place ejaculations one has to hear every day, I know not; but one thing I do know, their name is legion. They form a conspicuous part of our every-day language. They act something the part that a clown does at a circus—the fool. A fool is one destitute of sense. And surely none will contend that there is any sense in those thousand good-for-nothing words and phrases to which I refer. We ought to strike the whole family of these lingual monstrosities from our vocabularies of usable words. They are incorrigible vulgarisms, black spots on the fair face of our beautiful English—filthy vermin creeping among the clean garments of our thoughts. Why should we harbor them? What are they worth? Of what use are they? Whom do they benefit? Who likes us any the better for using them? Who regards them as an evidence of either wit, sense, or refinement? What ear do they please? To what taste do they administer? What sense do they gratify? Young gentlemen, young ladies, do you think they add any thing to the dignity of your character, to the refinement of your manners, the intelligence of your minds, the virtue of your hearts, or your general standing among intelligent, worthy people? Can you give any respectable, any decent apology, any one of which you yourselves would not be ashamed for their use? Then why use them? Why not cut them out of your conversation, your language; at once determine to use none but chaste, pure, sensible words—words which express clearly and forcibly your thoughts, which are evidences of inward purity and a refined taste—even the beautiful words of wisdom, which are like "apples of gold in pictures of silver?"

There is still one other evil use of language to which I

wish to refer. I mean profane swearing. I should be glad to speak at length upon this point, but must content my self with brevity. Of all useless, worthless, totally good for-nothing, and totally depraved habits, to which men bow in willing, voluntary bondage, the habit of profane swearing heads the list, and crowns the whole. For nearly all evil habits there can be some apology offered, some faint semblance of an excuse, some dim outline of the shadow of a reason, but for this I have never heard the first feeble attempt at a defense. This stands out a monstrous deformity in human language, with none to plead for its life or tell a single merit due to its being. In the use of profane language, no idea is to be expressed, no object is to be attained, no end secured, no ear to be pleased, no taste to be gratified, no friendship to be obtained, no appetite to be administered to, no passion to be fed, no title to be acquired, no wealth to be earned, no possible good, either real or imagined, is had in view. "Of all sinners," says a wise man, "profane swearers serve the devil for less wages than any other class." Indeed, they serve for nothing and find themselves, run their own risks, and make their own repairs at that. Mean service indeed, it would seem, that was not worth the poor pay of some pretended good. No one will pretend that there is any *wisdom* in profane swearing, for its words are not used to express ideas or convey thoughts, or impart instruction, or inspire meditation. No such thing as this is thought of. They are not designed, when spoken, for any such offices. They are used, as are all by-words, in consequence of a lack of wisdom, a want of good sense, to supply the place of ideas. They mean nothing. Surely no one would use them if he had ideas that he thought worth expressing, in their place. In consequence of a scarcity of ideas, these profane words are thrown in, to keep up the sound and give the appearance of thoughts. They are wicked cheats, playing a game of deception, attempting to palm off a blustering sound for a substantial thought. Profanity is surely a good witness of a terrible dearth of wisdom, a frightful scarcity of ideas. Nor will any one pretend that there is any good in profanity; for besides being an arrant cheat, it is an idle and wicked use of the names of the greatest and best Being in the universe, the best and truest friend of every human creature. In this no one can believe there is any good. It breeds contempt for God, for His sacred name, for all holy things. It outrages the best and holiest feelings of our moral natures, our reverence for Deity, and our gratitude to the best friend we have, for unnumbered favors. It blunts the moral sensibilities, and confounds all our ideas of justice, goodness, and gratitude. It moreover offends the ears of our best earthly friends, God's holiest and loveliest men and women, and sends a thrill of anguish through their hearts. Surely no one can dream of there being good in it. It is a totally evil thing. Neither will any one contend that it is courteous, or civil, or polite, or gentlemanly. It is opposed to all ideas of courtesy, to all rules of politeness, to all regulations for gentlemanly behavior.

Every one would be most heartily ashamed of himself

should he, by an unlucky slip of the tongue, use profane words in a refined circle of acquaintances.

The utter good-for-nothingness and silliness of profane swearing is well shown in the anecdote of a good Quaker. He had by some accident offended one of his neighbors. The neighbor, to vent his wrath, wrote him a long and most terribly profane letter, being about half made up of profane words. The good Quaker wrote him a very mild reply, of about the same length, in which he interspersed very thickly, in parenthesis, the phrase, "*bottles* and *tongs*," to supply the place of his neighbor's profanity. Now, if all profane swearers would do as the Quaker did, use the phrase "bottles and tongs," instead of profane words, they would see what a pigmy atom of sense is found in profane swearing, and what a terrible outrage of pure language it is. I can not dwell upon this subject. But, before I close, permit me to urge it upon every young man who has ever indulged in the wicked and worthless habit of profanity, or any thing that looked like it, to think seriously upon the subject, before he ever profanes the name of his God, or wounds the ears of his most refined friends, or defiles the purity of our beautiful English again. It is a sin against God, a sin against man, and a sin against the chastity of language. Let it be viewed in its proper light. Our thoughts we should prize too highly, and respect too deeply, to deform their dress with the deformity of profanity or any other vulgarism. We dress our bodies with good care and taste. We decorate and adorn them. Are not our thoughts of much more value? Whatever adornments we may give our physical bodies, let us not fail to attire our thoughts in the most chaste and tasteful garments, and adorn them with the most refined beauties of language. Let us adorn them with the beautiful words of chaste and refined sentiment, which are like apples of gold in pictures of silver.

LECTURE XI.

CULTIVATION OF THE INTELLECT

General Adoration of Intellectual Capacity—Creative Power of Intellect—Uncultivated Intellect has few Pleasures—Cultivated Intellect Grasps the Universe—Geniuses of the Past—Mind Immortal—Mental Culture Progressive—Culture gives Power to do Good—Knowledge is Power—How shall the Poor be Educated—Poverty a Mental Stimulant—The Will is the Way—Poverty a good Schoolmaster—Glory of Cultivated Intellect.

From time immemorial intellectual endowments have been crowned with bays of honor. In all times and nations intellect has been the idol-god of the human race. Men have worshiped at its shrine with an Eastern idolatry. Men of great intellect have been regarded as demi-gods. The multitude have looked upon them with awe-struck wonder. An impression has been felt as of the presence of a grand and solemn agent of spiritual majesty and power. With cheerful and reverent hands the world has crowned intellect with its richest honors. Its pathway has been strewn with flowers; its brow has worn the loftiest plume; it has sat upon the proudest throne; it has held the mightiest scepter of power. This general, universal adoration of intellect is proof at once, both of its transcendent worth and power. But evidences mightier than these are standing thick as stars in night's diadem all through the universe, proclaiming the worth and power of that which produces thought, and adapts ends to means.

By intellect Divine came the earth, rolling her vast circuit among the numberless hosts of the family of worlds, with all its rich and gorgeous furniture. By intellect came the glory-flashing magnificence of heaven, its blazing suns lit beyond suns that roam and shine through the measureless spaces of immensity. By intellect human came the secondary creations that mark with the chiseled lines of thought and skill the career of man—the cultivated fields, the vine-clad hills, the mill-strewn vales, the love-lit homes, the village-decked plains, the city-girt continents, the steamer-covered streams, the wire-woven and iron-bound lands, and sail-wreathed oceans. By intellect came all the stirring, sublime, mystery-woven realities of the universe. Then is it not worthy of our attention? And though but a feeble spark be ours, should it not be cultivated?

But again. In our daily avocations, our chase for wealth, our ambitious struggles for honor, our journeyings for happiness, in the direction of our social and benevolent movements, the establishment of governments and their multiform concomitants; in the formation of our characters and the solution of our life-problems on the world's great theater of action, intellect is our guide. It is our "cloud by day and our pillar of fire by night," hung above our pathway, to lead us by its light. It is our sole dependence, to plan, design, direct, determine, and decide in and upon all questions, actions, matters, and things that concern us as living, sentient, and accountable beings. In all things, from planting a potato to evolving a philosophy, intellect is our guide. Its decisions are our law, its voice is our teacher, its authority is the supreme judgment to which we must bow. Then should it not claim our care, our most careful hand of cultivation?

Once more. Intellect uncultivated has but few pleasures, and those are low and gross. But the pleasures of cultivated intellect are among the most refined and noble as well as the most ecstatic that enter into and form a part of human happiness. To the man of truly cultivated power of thought there are a thousand voices that speak the rich language of instruction and wisdom, to which the uncultivated ear is totally deaf. He passes not only all the common enjoyments of life, home, friends, the bounties and beauties of munificent nature, in a degree greatly elevated by his cultivation, but he holds within his hands the keys that unlock the grandest treasures of the universe, and give him permission to walk the heights of glory where angels tread. To him the sun pours down his glory wreathed beams of warmth and life, laden with the rich instructions which science teaches of that glorious illuminator and governor of the solar system. Every ray is a dispatch from that gorgeous world of light, speaking of its opake body, its vast magnitude, its luminous atmosphere, its revolutions on its own axis, its mighty attractive powers, its distance from us, the mysterious and almost godlike influence which it exerts upon our earth, the life and beauty it infuses into all things nere, and all the rich and varied instruction gleaned by the penetrating mind of man from this sunsource of light. The stars bring to him intelligence from the regions they inhabit, and each constellation affords him historic information of those who have gazed upon its stellar beauty in centuries gone by. The comets come to him on rapid wings of light, with their banners streaming back, telling by their inconceivable velocities, of the measureless depths they have penetrated in the immensity of the Creator's realm. The moon pours down its floods of light, freighted with its burden of knowledge. The clouds come over him but to tell him the story of their vapor-wreaths and the mission they have to perform. The lightnings flash but to give him instructive joy. The thunders rattle but to make him music. The winds roar but to whistle in his ears the story of their lives and labors. The earthquake moans but to send a voice of instruction from below, and the volcano flashes up its flames, a great torchlight to read earth's ancient history by. Old ocean pronounces in his ears its solemn sermon of grandeur, and the plains and mountains send back their instructive responses. The little flower beneath his feet opens its roseate volume to his admiring gaze; the blade of grass translates its mystical language for his pleasure, and the delicate leaf breathes about him its silent words of wisdom.

He finds instruction in the cattle upon the thousand hills, in the birds above him, and the fishes below him. He finds "books in running brooks, sermons in stones," and a voice in every thing bidding him to a great feast of intellectual pleasure. Yet more than this. It is his to be surrounded by the greatest and best minds which have reared their monumental piles upon the soil of intellect, as his compan ions. The blind old bard of Scio relates to him the story of his Grecian heroes. The immortal Tully speaks to him the words of fire and flame, of thought and power, which rang in Roman ears, and made his name the imperishable thing it is. Milton spreads before him the wings of hi' lofty imagination. Shakspeare opens the human heart to his view. Byron makes a bonfire of human passions foı his delight. Melancthon and Luther tell him of the great Reformation. The northman, Swedenborg, takes the vail from the human soul and shows its spirituality; while German Goethe and Schiller reveal its aesthetical powers. Bailey sketches for him, in words now of broken rock, and anon of flute-like melody, the strange mutations of human life. Hemans sings to him of love and faith, and all the great, and all the good, and all the wise gather around him to increase the sources of his pleasure. Now he may listen to the eloquence of a pious divine touching duty, heaven, and God, and anon trace the history of the church of Christ. Great is the joy of such a companionship. Most gratifying is such a communion of soul with the minds of the great and good. Rich, deep, and pure are the pleasures of cultivated intellect. Only a few of them have we enumerated, and those in the most feeble manner. They can not well be told. They are to be *felt.* Is not, then, the cultivation of our intellects an object worthy of our atten tion?

But another thought comes here, a great and glorious one, one that sparkles instruction, and we might almost say works by inspiration, wherever it goes. It is that mind is immortal, and that all its real adornments of wisdom and knowledge are put on for an endless state of existence. The transcendent powers of thought which man possesses were not made for a day, but for eternity. They will live when all perishable things shall have passed away. They shall be blooming in youth when the sun and stars are hoary with age. They will live to witness the transformation of all material forms, the wreck of matter, and the crush of worlds; live to see the passing away of the old heavens and earth, and the establishment of new and more glorious ones. The treasures of memory locked in the archives of intellect, must be immortal. The thoughts which spring into being within us leave imperishable mementoes behind. Mind leaves this world, freighted with all its wealth, for the great ocean of endless life. The thought-pearls which we gather along the journey of life are treasures for eternity. The intellectual cultivation of earth is for heaven. Every mental improvement we make here is not only an improvemeut for time, but for eternity. The adornments of mind are our sources of pleasure hereafter as well as here, and increase our happiness in heaven as well as on earth. Then, I ask, emphatically, is not the intellect worthy of a life-long cultivation?

Still another thought claims a moment's attention.

Intellectual cultivation is a progressive work. The powers of the mind unfold with their exertion. Each successive effort adds to its power. Every new thought gleaned from the voyage of life confers upon it a new strength. Every struggle for truth, every effort for a clearer light, every strife for a noble victory, every press against the barriers of life, or the adverse currents of earth, every resistance of error, every toil-earned discovery, every soul-rack and drop of brain-sweat adds something to the power, brilliancy, and treasury of the intellect. And as it progresses in the great life before it, its capacities for higher attainments are augmented, its vision is made clearer, its perceptions more lucid, its reflections more just, its comprehension more enlarged, its pleasures more deep and ecstatic, until it shall reach that point of intellectual grandeur and power attained by angelic beings, until it shall comprehend the mighty thoughts that revolve in their minds, and feel the transcendently glorious pleasures which glow in their souls. The more rapid our intellectual cultivation, the sooner these sublime attainments will be realized, and the sooner we shall reach the high plains of celestial glory occupied by the children of light. Then most earnestly do I press the question, is not intellectual cultivation an object worthy of our deepest consideration?

Bear with me a little longer on this part of my subject, while I present a thought or two more.

The cultivated intellect is a source of never-failing pleasure to its friends and companions. It is a mine of wealth sparkling with instruction. It has an attractive force, which draws around itself the minds of others, and delights them with its companionship. Its words are rich with the magic power of thought. It charms the ear with its varied harmony of rich and glowing language. It ravishes the heart with its recitals of the poetry of passion and love. It fires the imagination with the flights of its fancy, and the gorgeous drapery of its figures. It captivates the judgment by the justness of its opinions, the cogency of its reason, and the comprehensiveness of its views. Who that has ever enjoyed the companionship of a truly cultivated intellect, knows not its power to please and instruct the mind, to captivate and ravish the heart? How full of interest is the conversation of a truly intelligent man or woman! How eagerly do we seek the company of such, and how long do we enjoy it before we tire! Great are the charms which the cultivated intellect has for its companions. Then shall we not cultivate ours?

Again, the cultivation of intellect increases our abilities to do good. Is a nation oppressed with tyranny? Are unjust laws grinding the face of the poor? Are existing institutions opposed to the well-being of the masses of the people? Are old errors blinding the public mind and vailing the soul of humanity from the light of truth? Is ignorance palsying human energies and dwarfing human powers? Is the whirlpool of intemperance swallowing up its thousands? Is war and slavery cursing their millions? Cultivated intellect must apply the Archimedean lever of reform to these ruinous evils, or they can never be removed. Shall we then cultivate ours?

Is the world to be reformed, improvements to be made, laws to be enacted, governments to be framed, institutions to be established, discoveries made, education carried to the masses, charity applied to the unfortunate, justice administered, diseases cured, science taught, religion proclaimed to a sinful world? Cultivated intellect must perform these Herculean tasks.

Once more. In the ordinary avocations of life, in attempting to live by the Golden Rule, in practicing the religion of Christ, in striving to realize in our lives the great idea of the common brotherhood, in living for our families, our country, and our race, we are greatly assisted by the cultivation of our intellectual powers. I would that my young readers could realize the importance of this thought. Our ability to do good is in proportion to the degree of cultivation our minds have received, other things being equal. This is the thought. It is an important one. If it could be realized by the young, it is certain that they would put forth their noblest efforts for the cultivation of their mental powers. If they really desire the good of their fellows, if they wish to see the world reformed of its evils, if they would be instruments in the hands of God of blessing the human kind, they can not fail to endeavor to increase their ability to engage successfully in every good work. If they would have power for righteousness-sake over their fellows, they must acquire it by the cultivation of their intellects. There is a power in a single cultivated mind which a thousand ignorant ones can never wield. It is a common saying, that "knowledge is power," but it is not so much knowledge, as it is the cultivation which the obtaining of that knowledge has conferred upon the mind that possesses it. There is a hidden, but great power, in every cultivated mind. It is ready to plan, and fruitful in expedients to execute. Whoever then would wield an in fluence over his fellows, let him cultivate his mind.

But above all these considerations, there is still another higher, stronger, holier. Intellect is the gift of God, and in respect for Him should be cultivated with the greatest assiduity. He gave it, with the command to water, prune and cultivate it. "Bury not thy talent in the earth," is His impressive mandate. Who will obey His will? Who will show that they honor the name of their Father by sowing in the soil of the intellect the seeds of wisdom and truth, and cultivating them with industrious care?

But here some one may ask, How shall I cultivate my intellect? I am poor, and have not the means to procure an education. *Have not the means!* Has poverty robbed you of a single intellectual power? Has it not sharpened them all? Has it shut you out from nature, from truth, and from God? Has it taken away from you the glorious objects of thought which the Creator has spread around you in grand and solemn profusion? Has it broken the silken cord that binds you to your fellows? Has it shut out the brilliant creations of their minds from yours? Has it palsied your senses? Has it forbid that you should gaze into the solemn, yet sparkling depths of your own soul and read there the treasures of wisdom which God has written, never to be erased? Has it sealed the book of your own heart? Nay, verily. All that is great, good, beautiful, sublime and glorious, is yet yours. You are robbed of nothing. You are yet God's freeborn child, with the boundless riches of your paternal inheritance about you. Your powers are unimpaired. They are beautiful and strong as ever. Why then not cultivate them? Why does poverty prevent? Money will not buy you study, or thought, or mental strength. You can think, reason, meditate, without money. You can exercise all your faculties upon all the objects around you, without money. Wealth will not convert a dunce into a genius. Gold will not store the mind with wisdom; more likely it will fill it with folly. It may decorate your body, but it can not adorn your soul. Strange thought, that money will cultivate your intellect. You are mad to entertain a thought so absurd. The poorer you are, the easier it is for you to cultivate your mind. You have more and greater stimulants to action, and fewer inducements to idleness and folly. It is hard for the rich youth to cultivate his mind or heart. Much more favorable and preferable are the opportunities of the poor. From among the poor have come the great majority of the world's greatest and best characters.

But you say now, that you have not *time.* Not time to *think!* How can you help thinking? Not time to study! How can you avoid studying? Your mind is active, ever active, ever thinking, ever studying. All you have to do is to direct it to proper objects, and in proper channels, and it will cultivate itself. You have time enough for nonsense, idleness, waste, gossip, foolery, but not time enough to cultivate your mind. Whoever lives to thirty years of age without cultivating his mind, is guilty of an enormous waste of time. The truth is, there is nothing to prevent but a *will.* Whoever forms a resolute determination tc cultivate his mind will find nothing in his way. If he finds barriers, they will only make him stronger in surmounting them. Every thing will administer to his progress in the great work. Aids will come from every quarter. Teachers will gather around him in numberless hosts. The air will breathe notes of instruction, and running brooks give him lessons of wisdom. The bee, the worm, the bird, the rock, the cloud, the ocean, the heavens above him, will read him lectures on science. Light and darkness, heat and cold, every thing in nature, life the human soul, will gather around him with a voice of instruction, as soon as he determines to be instructed. He can walk a lifetime amid all these things, and get no instruction. But as soon as he begins to look for it, it begins to come. The great Audubon spent half his life in the forests looking at the birds. One great man spent the most of his life studying spiders. Others have studied among snakes, lizards, bugs, and worms, and have found infinite delight in their pursuits. Some have studied the stars, others the flowers, and others the rocks. Learn this truth, young man and woman: "*The will is the way.*" Form that, and the gardens of your minds will be thoroughly cultivated. It is not necessary that a fortune shall be spent to afford you the opportunities of schools and colleges. These are invaluable aids. But life, the world, may become one great school, and every thing therein a teacher. The mind may be cultivated without schools, thoroughly, deeply cultivated without them.

Moreover, any young man or woman, with ordinary health

and powers of mind, can obtain with his or her exertions all the advantages afforded in the most excellent schools of our day. The heart to do will afford the needed means. Let them dispense with superfluities both in dress and living, eat and wear only what is necessary for health and comfort, and apply their earnings in attending school. Let them earn a few dollars, then spend it in this way; then earn more, and use it in the same way; and they will soon find themselves in the possession of cultivated minds. In the ordinary avocations of life the mind may be cultivated. In the very pursuit of the means to attend school the young may cultivate their minds.

The youth who believes it impossible for him to get an education, is deficient in courage or energy. The youth who will stay away from the feast of knowledge because he is poor, is a coward or a ninny. Poverty is a good school to try powers. Experience has taught me this lesson.

Look out upon the world, and see what a fearful waste of barren, desolate, lifeless intellect there is around us. It is awful to behold. Young, brave, noble, immortal minds are growing up in blank darkness. Their young powers are rusting within them. A fearful shadow hangs over them. Their mental blindness makes angels weep. The uncultivated wastes of their souls present a sad picture for a benevolent heart to behold. And, what makes it sadder, they are not aware of their own utter barrenness. They feel not their own palsy of mind. Shall it be always so? Will not the youth of this generation improve upon the last? The age demands it. The promise of the future demands it. The hopes of the great aud good, the spirit of benevolence, humanity, and God demand it. Yes, and another demand comes pressing its claims upon us for it. It comes from the depths within. Our own souls demand it. Their happiness, their exaltation, their present and everlasting good, their standing in life and in the bright retinue of angels, demand a thorough and life-long cultivation of the powers of their own minds. There is no describing the power, majesty, and glory of a cultivated intellect. Human language has no powers for such an office. The dialect above alone can tell what is permitted us now only to conceive.

Let us be wise, my youthful readers, and visit daily the treasure-caves of thought. Let us turn in to the chambers within us, and decorate them with the pictures of the mental brush and pencil. Our minds are our God-given inheritance. Let us improve them well, that we may hear within us the applauding voice, "Well done, thou good and faithful servant."

LECTURE XII.

CULTIVATION OF THE MORAL SENTIMENTS.

Moral Sentiments, the Imperial Crown of the Human Soul—Moral Culture necessary—Immortality, the Glory of Man's Being—Alliance of Man with his Maker—Adversity Fortifies the Soul—Moral Force the Fruit of Trial—The Storms and Trials of Life—Moral Power Invulnerable—The Five Moral Jewels—Veneration—Link between God and Man—Benevolence—Power and Scope of Benevolence—Conscientiousness—Hope—Fraternity of the Moral Affections—Faith, or Spiritual Light—Result of Moral Culture.

I COME in this lecture to speak of the imperial crown of the human soul, the *moral capacities* with which God has endowed it. In this crown are set five jewels, more beautiful than the stars, lovely in the sight of angels, and precious in the eye of God—love to God, love to man, the love of truth and right, hope, and spiritual perception. Viewed in his intellectual capacity, man is a being of vast and varied powers, rising up before us like a tall son of light, with a vision possessing at once the two extremes of optical perception; with his microscopic power viewing the infinitesimal minutiæ of the wonderful creation about him, and with his telescopic eye stretching away into the cerulean depths of the star-built universe, to revel amid its ceaseless wonders; now examining the physiological structure of an insect, or unfolding the life and history of the infusoria about it; now discovering a world, and reading the statute book of God concerning its governments; and now, with a gigantic stretch of thought, taking in a sweep of myriad worlds.

Viewed in his affectionate capacities, as a social being, he is interesting and amiable, loving with a strange and undefinable tenderness the objects related to him by kindred or congenial ties; sacrificing ease, strength, health, time, life, all, upon the altar of his affections. But viewed as a moral being, he rises infinitely higher, and appears related to angels and God. Now the virtues take their places in his soul, and stand in shining ranks in the sunlight of duty. Goodness, charity, constancy, magnanimity, justice, adoration, hope, faith, are among the virtues of the moral man. These are the bright, rich fruits that spring in generous abundance from man's moral powers. These are the rays emitted from the jewels set in the diadem of his soul. These are the flowers that bloom in this moral garden of the man within. If there is any beauty in them, any sanctity, any odor of heaven, any of the elixir of spiritual life; if they confer any peace upon his heart, any light upon life's pathway, any joy upon the being within, any glory upon the soul, they should be cultivated, cultivated much, with care, with zeal, with deep and earnest devotion.

In the moral nature of man are found the strongest evidences of his immortality, of the ever-increasing beatitudes of glory which its capacities fit him to attain, and which are revealed in the sacred Scriptures as the destiny de signed by God for His earthly children. This thought is a great and glorious one, and should not be lost. The idea of immortal existence, blessed with the progressive attainments most calculated to advance its happiness and dignify and adorn its being, is one that the moral nature of man has ever delighted to cherish. When we think of the moral man, as existing through all future ages, beyond the shores of time and the dominion of death, as surviving the earth and sky, as living when the magnificence of the material universe shall have faded away, as exempted from every error and imperfection of its present state of being, as clothed upon with a higher life and an angel's glory, as realizing the beatitudes of an immortal and glorified state, as elevated with the most lofty conceptions of the wide universe of being around it, designed to shed light along the line of its immortal destiny, and spread everywhere the glory of God; when we think of it, as rejoicing in the wisdom and power of an intellectual strength, which comprehends the loves, order, and harmony of spiritual being; the objects, and uses, and relations of the material universe, in developing the highest excellences of the soul; as having an access to the minds of the wise and good of all times and nations, and enjoying their companionship, as an immortal flow of soul and feast of reason; when we think of it as sanctioning innumerable friendships with beings of rich and varied attainments, of singular intellectual capacities, and a loftiness of virtue of which we can now have but the least possible conception; as cherishing an affection for the great and good, whose names have adorned the pages of history, and enjoying their society and lofty conversation; as delighting in a universal love for the children of God, and exulting in the companionship with Christ, and an intercourse with God more familiar than the closest intimacy of earth has ever shadowed forth; when we thus think of the coming and eternal life of man, in which his moral sentiments are to be his crowning glory; in which they are to give him his chief dignity and importance as an immortal being, and which are to unite him with all glorified beings, and with the eternal throne of that Great Being who is clothed with all majesty and power, we can not but be awed into a deep and holy respect for this part of our common nature, and feel that no duty is so imperious and pressing as that which bids us cultivate the moral powers of our souls. In considering our duties, we are too apt to forget what manner of beings we are. We look through the eyes of time and sense. We permit our visions to be contracted by the boundaries of what is visible. We forget the greatness of our natures and the majesty of our moral powers. We forget that for just such beings as we are the earth was made, with all its splendid furniture; the sky, with all its radiant worlds; that for us the upper world has lavished its treasures; that for us the Son of God, the Lord of Life and Glory, has labored, bled, and died. We forget that we are allied to the greatest and best men and women that have ever lived, to angels, to Christ, and to God. True, we are sinful and comparatively degraded. Looked upon in his worst estate, in his debaucheries, crimes, and wars, man would almost appear an incarnation of evil. But look a little closer, and it will be seen that even here the true majesty of his nature may be seen. For here will be seen struggles against temptations, efforts at resistance of evil, resolutions for high purposes, desires for a better life, and hopes of some good yet unattained, which speak of the soul's inborn capacities. Here, too, it will be found, are nourished some of earth's noblest virtues, as well as loftiest and purest spirits. Washington was made the great and pure man he was, as much by the crying wickedness of his times as by the native grandeur of his soul. The stern, wicked rigors of Europe's penal code developed the virtues that gave the world a Howard. As the strong oak is made mightier by the storms that heap against it, as the arm becomes stalwart and powerful by repeated strokes, so do virtues grow in the soul, by the struggles at resistance, occasioned by the wickedness of the world.

Patience, that lovely, serene, summer-heaven virtue, which imparts to its possessor the mien and sweetness of an angel, is born and nourished amid trials, perplexities, and spirit-struggles. Resignation is the fruit of sorrow. Faith is the flower of need. Mercy is the angel form that sin reveals, to sweeten its bitterness and melt away its hardness. Moral courage and force are reared amid temptation and the besetments of evil; so that man, even in his sins, exhibits the moral grandeur of his soul, and shows us not only the necessity but the importance and worth of moral cultivation. If we really felt the worth of our own powers, if we appreciated the beings we call ourselves, far otherwise than they are would be our lives.

If we comprehended the progressive developments of virtue and spiritual excellence which we are capable of attaining, the moral power which we may inspire within ourselves, we should be far more sensible than we are of the duties which we owe the moral man.

The great end to be attained in the cultivation of the moral powers, is moral force, spiritual energy of soul, to be and do what to us is most desirable for a high, immortal, moral, and accountable being. As we are, we fail to please ourselves; we fall below our own standard; we yield to temptations, when we desire not so to do; we are unguarded at times, when we have need of being strong; we often find our citadel exposed, when we feel no power to defend it. In these emergencies, to which all moral beings in the earth find themselves driven, we have need of an inward strength, a moral power of soul, which will enable us to resist the encroachments of evil. There are times in the lives of us all, when the soul shrinks back in weakness and dismay, before the burdens laid before it to bear. It looks, in heart-sickness and despair, upon the cross it must take up. When friends desert us; when scandal points her envenomed darts at the reputation we have earned in struggles and hopes; when fortunes, acquired in the sweat and toil of years, take wings and flee away; when the dearest and longest cherished hopes of the heart are crushed by the chill hand of disappointment; when beloved ones, that live in our very souls, are snatched from our embraces, and are borne off in the icy arms of death; when any severe affliction or trial is laid upon us, we feel our inability to bear it; we give way to despondency, we shrink back into the gloomy solitudes of despair, too weak to meet the solemn messenger of adversity face to face, too nerveless to stand up under our burdens, and give God thanks for our trials, intended to confer the strength of soul we need, and fit us for higher modes of spiritual life. Then it is that we feel our moral weakness; then it is that the prayer for an inward, angelic energy of soul goes up in deep and solemn earnestness to God; then it is that we are most dissatisfied with ourselves, and feel the necessity of higher moral attainments than we have yet acquired. We can not be prepared for these trials, which we must meet, without due attention to the cultivation of our moral powers. I would that my young friends could be made to realize the importance of this subject. Life is a stormy sea. They are yet in the harbor of youth. The winds that rush across the mighty main sweep not against them; the waves that roll in the broad sea break not over them. But the time will surely come when the storm-clouds will gather and the thunders rattle, when the sea will rock and the sails of life will be rent, when the heart will sink in despair and the soul cry out in wretchedness. It is for such seasons that we have need to be prepared; it is in such times that we have need of elevated and cultivated moral powers. I know not that at such times they are of more value to us than in seasons of prosperity; but then we *feel* their importance more, and it is then that the beauty and grandeur of our moral attainments shed their holiest luster in the soul, and become to us as the rainbow after the storm. There is something in moral excellence so beautiful, so truly adorable, that all beings with a spark of moral perception fall down and worship before it. There is something in it so pure, so holy, so kindred with heaven, so nearly allied to God, that it inspires all moral beings with a feeling of its divinity. The man who is calm amid dangers, pure and holy amid temptations, firm when other hearts are quaking, honest when he has no watcher but his conscience and his God, who gives his best alms in secret, and breathes his intensest devotions in the closet of his own soul; who obeys his convictions of right when he knows the world will denounce; whose religious trust forsakes him never, and in whose breast there is a moral power, a voice, a Christ, which says to his soul in the midnight of the storm of adversity and affliction, "Peace, be still!" this man is one to whom all hearts bow in respect; one whom all men delight to honor, and is truly the noblest work of God. It is this moral power that we ought to strive to attain. We ought to be capable of forming resolute determinations to good, and living by these resolutions, as irrevocable rules of life. Nothing else so elevates and honors the young as the possession of such moral energies. No other adornment is half so beautiful, no other crown is half so honorable and bright. It rests on the brow of youth like a rainbow on the front of a cloud, and gives promise of a glorious life. Then let all youth strive for this coronal of glory, that the fruits of honor, peace, and spiritual life, may grow abundantly in their souls.

But I remarked in the outset of this discourse that there were five jewels set in this crown, to blend their radiance in one, to illuminate the pathway of life. It is proper that I should speak briefly of these. And, first and brightest of all, is *Veneration*, that moral link that binds man most closely with his God; that spiritual garden, where the creature walks in sweet companionship with his Maker; that feeling which adores, worships, loves the Divine Being, and which clings to Him with a holy, a devout, and reverential affection. This is the central, all-radiant sun-jewel, set in the crown of the soul. Its light is pure, heavenly, tranquilizing, and spiritualizing. The sentiment of veneration, of worship, of love to the Divine Being, is the highest, the holiest, noblest, and most truly sublime, that man is capable of cherishing. It has for its object the perfection of the Godhead. It fixes its regards upon the immortal glories of the great Father of lights. It binds itself to a Being fitted, as no other being is, to impart to the soul the highest moral grandeur that created beings can attain. It communes with the omnipotent spirit of love, which transfuses its energies throughout the wide creation. It is the upper window of the soul which opens into the clear, radiant light of God's eternal home. It is the ladder of Jacob, on which angels ascend and descend in intimate intercourse between the soul and its God It is an affection, a love as positive, as real, as warm, as imperative in its demands for activity, as any implanted in our natures. It is the grandest and noblest affection of the soul, because it fixes its regards upon the sublimest and holiest object in the universe. And its influence in every department of the mind is more salutary and holy than any other, because of the strength of the feeling and the nature of the Being upon which its adoration is fixed. As God is holier, lovelier than any other being, the affection for Him is more excellent in its influence upon the mind than any other. No mind can be perfect, no other affection can rise to its highest degree of perfection, no faculty to its most exalted state, without the sanctifying power of this sentiment. If we would perfect our natures, if we would exalt our affections, if we would ennoble our souls, if we would reach the acme of true human greatness, we must give to the sentiment of veneration its full and perfect influence in our minds. It is the basis of religion; it is the religious feeling. It is opposed to all evil, opposed to the undue exercise of any and every faculty. Its will is the will of God, so far as it knows the divine desire. It is opposed to all things which militate against the laws and precepts of the Most High. It loves obedience to God. It delights in dependence upon Him. It sees His hand in every created thing. It feels Him everywhere, and rejoices in the feeling. It offers praise and thanksgiving. It lifts itself in prayer. It bows itself in worship. It venerates God and all things kindred with Him. It loves holiness, loves purity in thought and life; loves devotedness to truth and right; loves sincerity, sanctity of spirit; loves the highest virtues; loves goodness, humility, meekness, love. In fine, it loves all things upon which God smiles. It should be one of the primary and principal objects of all persons, and especially of the young, to cultivate this affection; to direct its energies to the one living and true God; to inspire it with all possible power; to enkindle all its holy fires; to spread its sanctifying charm through all the faculties of the soul. Its natural language is praise and prayer. It delights to make known its love to the one object of its regard. In this respect it is like any other affection. All affection is communicative, and delights, above every thing else, to make itself known to the object on which it fixes its attention. It delights in praises of that object, in expressions of its respect and attachment. It never wearies in imparting itself, in making known the depth and strength of the fires within. Hence, praise and prayer is the natural language of veneration. These inspire it with power and activity. These enkindle its fires. These give it cultivation. Religious worship augments its activities. Sanctuary exercises awaken its powers. Religious associations give permanency to its feelings. Hence, public and private worship, religious meetings and exercises of all kinds, are profitable for the cultivation of this, the highest faculty of the human soul. All religious ceremonies and exercises were established, and are supported, by this sentiment. They are the visible expression of its office and power. Their atmosphere is the element in which it delights to live. So that we see that religion, worship, praise, prayer, devotion, are as natural as they are revealed. All this is the voice of this sentiment, speaking out its own nature, and reminding us of its great Author.

I have not time to speak more upon this faculty, which is the crowning glory of the human mind. But permit me to urge its cultivation upon my young friends, as one of the most sacred duties of life. Neglect it not. Neglect not the sanctuary. Neglect not religious reading, religious reflections, the formation of religious opinions, and the cultivation of a religious life. The highest beauties of your souls, the finishing touch of your characters, the sweetest charm of your lives will be given, by due attention to this, your first and last duty.

The second jewel set in the mental coronal, is *Benevolence*, the love of our fellow, the humane, sympathetic feeling—that which seeks the good of others; that which would pour out from the treasures of its munificence gifts of good things upon all. It is that feeling that gave the world a Howard, a Fenelon, a Fry. It is that feeling that leads on the reformer, which inspires the philanthropist, which blesses, and curses not. It is the good Samaritan of the heart. It is that which thinketh no evil, and is kind; which hopeth all things, believeth all things, endureth all things. It is the angel of mercy which forgives seventy-and-seven times, and still is rich in the treasures of pardon. It visits the sick, smooths the pillow of the dying, drops a tear with the mourner, buries the dead, educates the orphan. It sets free the captive, unburdens the slave, instructs the ignorant, relieves the distressed, and preaches the gospel to the poor. Its look is like the face of an angel; its words are more precious than rubies; its voice is sweeter than honey; its hand is softer than down; its step as gentle as love. But I can not speak its praise. It needs no encomium; it is its own praise; its works are its plaudits. Whoever would be respected, whoever would be beloved, whoever would be useful, would be re membered with pleasure when life is over, must cherish this glorious feeling. Whoever would be truly happy, would feel the real charms of goodness, must cultivate this affection. It is a glorious affection, because of the number and extent of its objects. It is wide as the world of suffering, deep as the heart of sorrow, extensive as the wants of creation, and boundless as the kingdom of need. Its spirit is the messenger of peace, holding out to quarreling, sinning, wrangling mortals, the white flag of truce. It is needed everywhere, in all times and places, in all trades, professions, callings, which men can pursue with pleasure, profit, or honor. The world has too little of it. It has been neglected. It should now be cultivated much, and long, and well. The peace, the happiness, the prosperity of the world depends greatly upon it. Countries need it; communities need it; families need it; individuals need it. It is needed everywhere. Nothing gives a sweeter charm to youth than well-cultivated benevolence, an active charity, a disposition kind to all. Who can properly tell the power and sweetness of kindness? Would you possess them, my young friends? Then cultivate the benevolent dispositions of your natures. Fail not to do it. Let a glorious activity of universal love mark all your actions and feelings. Be kind, be good, be noble, be generous always. Let your words, your looks, your acts, breathe the spirit of love.

The third jewel is *Conscientiousness*—the love of truth and right. It is the spring-source of integrity. It has been said that an honest man is the noblest work of God. It is the inspiration of this sentiment which makes him such, which crowns him with his real nobility. A great writer has said, that the two most beautiful things in the material and mental creations are the "starry heavens and the sentiment of duty in the soul." A sentiment most noble and true. If there is a being beneath the government of the Most High, who is worthy of the heart's esteem and high respect; if there is one to whom my soul bows in willing reverence, and in whose presence I feel as though by the side of an angel; who awes me while he secures my love, it is he who has a strong, a ruling sense of duty in his heart. It appears to me as though there is something of God in the feeling. It works a divine inspiration upon me. It fills my soul with heavenly images, and binds my heart to its possessor. It has a ravishing charm, and works as though by miracle upon my inner senses. This sense of duty in the heart is inspired by conscientiousness. The ultimate of the authority and office of this sentiment is to impart this sense of duty. The idea of obligation, responsibility, faithfulness to trusts, rectitude, justice, right, is conferred by this faculty. The voice of this sentiment is for right. It has but one law written in the heart of its being, and that is the rule of right. It is a stern, noble representative in man of the attribute of justice in God. It is communicative, like other feelings and desires, imparting itself to others. It wishes to inspire its own glorious spirit everywhere, and make all hearts redolent of its light and the sanctity of heaven. It suffers in the presence of wrong, sorrows at injustice, weeps when any creature fails in duty. How much of sanctity, of holiness, of Godlike moral power this faculty, when strong, imparts to the human soul! It is the citadel of moral force, and should be guarded well. Faithfully should it be cultivated. Nothing should prevent a thorough and perpetual cultivation of this right arm of all morality. No luring bait of pleasure, no fancied interests, should prevent an active exercise of this spiritual power. Be assured, my young friends, that your real pleasure and interest are in harmony with this sentiment. Then, injure it never; outrage it never; question never its teachings. Be true to its voice, heed its warnings, obey its dictates, walk by its councils, comply with the letter and spirit of its law. Come what may, frown who will, hearken to the voice of duty. It is God in the soul, speaking a language beautiful as the words of heaven. Oh, fail not to cultivate now and forever this love of truth and duty.

The fourth jewel in the crown which God has placed upon His creature man, is *Hope*. It is that angel within, which whispers of triumph over evil, of the success of good, of the victory of truth, of the achievements of right. "It hopeth all things." It is a strong ingredient of courage. It is the friend of virtue. It is the prophet of "a good time coming." Its prophecy is "good tidings of great joy, which shall be unto all people." Its religion is full of glorious anticipation. It believes in a full redemption. It is a general inspirer of all the moral feelings. To veneration it says, "All shall know the Lord, from the least unto the greatest." "The ends of the earth shal' remember and turn unto the Lord, and all the kindreds of the earth shall worship before Him." "Every knee shall bow in spiritual homage, and every tongue shall confess him Lord and give Him praise, to His everlasting glory." "Every creature which is in heaven, on the earth, under the earth, in the sea, and all that are in them, shall say, Blessing, and honor, and glory, and power, be unto Him that sitteth upon the throne, and to the Lamb forever." To Benevolence it says, "God is love." "He is good unto all, and His tender mercies are over all His works." "He is good to the unthankful and the unkind." "He is gracious, long suffering, keeping mercy for thousands." "His love shall triumph over hatred." "His goodness shall overcome all evil." "He will bless, and curse not." "He will love His enemies, till their enmity of heart shall die, and they shall become His willing children." "He has prepared a feast of fat things for all people, of wines on the lees, well refined. He will wipe away tears from off all faces, and will take away the rebuke of His people from off all the earth." "Be kind and good to all, for there is a good time coming, when the lamb and the lion shall lie down together, and a little child shall lead them; when spears shall be beaten into pruning-hooks, and swords into plow-shares, and men shall learn war no more." To Conscientiousness it says, "God will reward every man according to his works. He is truth, and lieth not. His truth shall run and be victorious. He will finish sin, make an end of transgression, and bring in everlasting righteousness." These are the religious sentiments of Hope, breathing everywhere the idea of victory. They are inspiring, ennobling, glorious. Its morality is equally inspiring, rich, and beneficent. It encourages all things good, great, noble. It whispers liberty to the slave, freedom to the captive, health to the sick, home to the wandering, friends to the forsaken, peace to the troubled, supplies to the needy, bread to the hungry, strength to the weak, rest to the weary, life to the dying. It has sunshine in its eye, encouragement on its tongue, and inspiration in its hand. Rich and glorious is hope, and faithfully should it be cultivated. Let its inspiring influence be in the heart of every youth. It will give strength and courage. Let its cheerful words fall ever from his tongue, and his bright smile play ever on its countenance. Entertain well this nymph of goodness. Cultivate well this ever-shining flower of the spirit. It is the evergreen of life, that grows at the eastern gate of the soul's garden.

The fifth jewel in the imperial crown is *Faith, or Spiritual Light.* It is the true prophet of the soul, and ever beholds a spiritual life, spiritual relations, labors, and joys. Its office is to teach man that he is a spiritual being, that he has an inward life enshrined in this material encasement, an immortal gem set now in an earthly casket. It assures man that he lives not for this life alone, but for another superior to this, more glorious and real. It teaches that God is a spirit, and seeks such to worship Him. It dignifies humanity with immortality. It dwells ever upon an unseen world, announcing always that unseen realities are eternal. Virtue, knowledge, wisdom, mercy, love, righteousness, and worship, are among its immortal, unseen realities. Lofty, dignified, transcendently glorious are its teachings, and equally so are its moral influences. It is a faculty of the human soul too much neglected. The things of time and sense, earth and sin, waste its energies and dim its sight. We are too carnal, too earthly. We cultivate not enough our spiritual senses. Let us be wise, O youth, and fail not to invigorate our spiritual parts. Life will smile in gladness, and eternity rejoice in glory, if we are faithful in this duty. Youth is the time to commence its cultivation. Youth's powers are pliant and easily trained. Let life be our great school for the cultivation of all our moral powers. Upon the moral sentiments we can not bestow too much attention. They are vastly important to our happiness and eternal good. We can not honor them with too much attention. We can not be too watchful of their good. It should be the end and object of our life to dignify and adorn them. Our peace, our happiness, our standing in the scale of being, depends upon the cultivation we give them. Let us, then, be faithful, and erect a noble temple of virtue, whose glittering pinnacles shall reach the skies, and whose apartments shall be the fit dwelling-places of angels.

LECTURE XIII

CULTIVATION OF THE AFFECTIONS.

Man's Sympathy with the Sentient Universe—Affection, the Motive Force of the Soul—Power of the Affections—Charm of Reciprocity—Omnipotence of Love—How to Cultivate the Affections—Moral Worth the Basis of enduring Love—Reverence for Moral Purity—Reason and Will, the Guide of Affection—Filial Affection—Trust only those who Love their Parents—Fraternal Affection—Love of Country—Universality of Home-Love—Patriotism—Philanthropy—Universal Brotherhood.

MAN is a being of singular and glorious affections. We read that "*God is* LOVE." We read also that man is formed in the image of God; in the similitude of his Maker. This is the voice of Revelation. Our own consciousness responds to its truthfulness. If God were not love, He could not have formed within us the perpetual fountains of affection which we feel sending forth their crystal tides, as though fed by a shoreless and fathomless ocean. If we were not formed in His image, we should not feel that dependence upon Him, and that interest in our fellow which is the glory of our being. Our affectionate consciousness is the most deep and thrillingly exquisite of any thing we feel or know. It is the first to develop itself in our natures, the longest to live, and the last to die. It is the most stirring emotions, the most potent energy of the human soul. It is both the basis and the dome of the temple of the spirit. We see it in the little child often breathing forth its spirit in sublime energy, causing it to sacrifice every little good, all its toys, its plays, its treasures, its joys, upon the shrine of young affection. We see it developing itself with each succeeding year, till in the season of youth it assumes a spiritual grandeur, which is singularly imposing and noble, after wielding its power over the most turbulent passions, and taming the most wayward and stormy energies that ever beat up their surges in the human soul. In middle age, its power is still more imperious and general, forming the grand disideratum for which men live, inspiring their hopes, quickening their actions, and electrifying their energies. In old age it is the sovereign ruler within; in all cases, when it has been duly cultivated, becoming the master feeling, swaying the soul as does the breeze the harp of silken strings. On the shrine of affection are laid the most glorious sacrifices that humanity offers. Their name is *Myriad legion.* In the hovel among the mountains, in the palace on the plains, in the cot by the brook, in the frescoed seat of luxury, in the abodes of the poor and in the mansions of the rich, among the dwellers of the icy North, and those of the sunnv South, on the lone islands of the sea, and the distant lands of blossom and song, we find the same native plant of affection growing luxuriantly; in all climes and in all places, a native everywhere, and an exotic nowhere. The Indian, in his stern, savage vigor, and wild, storm-like power, bows, a softened and subdued worshiper, at its shrine. The philosopher, in the great laboratory of nature, with her crucibles, her telescopes, her fires, and her laws scattered around him, forgets not to bring his daily gift to the shrine of the heart. The monarch of empires, the king of nations, the commander of armies, the conqueror of the world, never blots from his soul the immortal image of the God of love.

Affection is universal and almost omnipotent. It is the spring-source of nearly all of earth's joys and the occasion of much of its most poignant anguish. The fault with the world is not so much that there is not affection enough, but that it is not properly directed, not sufficiently cultivated, not duly controlled. All our affections should be subjected to enlightened wisdom. They are of themselves blind impulses, loving only because they can not help it, acting only because it is their nature to act, casting their fragrance upon every wind, only because they have the fragrance and know not how to retain it. The heart must love. It was made to love.

> "The heart, like the tendril, accustomed to cling,
> Let it grow where it will, can not flourish alone;
> But will lean to the nearest and loveliest thing
> It can twine with itself and make closely its own."

If, then, it must and will exercise its native and inborn powers, it is evident that it should be so directed and cultivated that its affections shall yield the greatest possible amount of joy, and the least possible amount of misery. The natural result of the peaceful exercise of the affections is happiness the most pure and thrilling. This is always the result, when they are not fixed upon unworthy objects, or fail in that reciprocity which they covet, in which lies their highest and most exquisite charm. The mother who wastes her affections upon her undutiful and unloving child, feels a pain more severe, arising from this want of reciprocity, than any other which it is possible for her to feel. So of every other affection. Its secret and all-glorious charm lies in its reciprocity. It is important, then, that every youth understand the true basis of affection, that in the formation of attachments, in the cultivation of friendships, in the choice of companions, he may be so guided by wisdom that all such affections shall yield the serene and heavenly charm of love, and be destitute of its thorn and its woe.

Attachments must be formed, friendship's golden chain must be forged, companions must be selected from the circle of youth's acquaintance. There is no avoiding this. Then the duty of every youth is to be wise, and love that, and only that, which is lovely; seek the companionship of that, and that only, which is good; choose for associates those, and those only, who are pure and worthy; trust those, and those only, who are honest; and cherish the affections of those, and those only, to whom the whole heart's confidence can be yielded without fear or mental reservation. The basis of all true and lasting affection is real *worth*, genuine mental excellence. He who loves, or confides in aught else, builds upon a sandy foundation, and must surely feel a wreck of heart and a blight of hopes. It can not last; for that upon which it is built must pass away, and with it must pass away the affection. But real worth is enduring. Mental and moral excellence is an eternal thing. It can not pass away. It is that which God loves. It is that which makes heaven the glorious place it is. It is that upon which angels base the transcendent love that enriches their hearts. It 's that which gives the robes of glory to the celestial inhabitants, that which crowns them with the diadem of immortal beauty. All affection, all friendship based upon this must be pure and enduring. It will grow deeper and purer with age, and strengthen with the increase of years. Every day will make it more heavenly, more sacred, more holy, and more happy in its spiritual results. Every day it will fill more and more all the chambers of the soul with sadness. Every day its radiance will be more soft and pure, and its influence more exalted and powerful. Its effects will be visible in all the life. It will teach the tongue to speak its own soft words of tenderness; it will mellow the voice to the cadences of harp-like music; it will give its own glorious summer radiance to the eye. It will wreathe itself in smiles all over the countenance, or flow in the dewy tears of sympathy. It will guide the feet in the way of righteousness. It will change the lusts to missionaries of purity and affectionate fervor; and inspire the whole soul with the life and beauty of its own celestial sweetness. These are its effects in life. But they go beyond. Eternity shall behold all the glory and blessedness of such affections. They shall be more bright and glorious in that world than in this. The soul that loves truly once, loves forever.

A friendship based upon *real worth* is an immortal thing. It will add as much to the glory and blessedness of heaven as it does to the happiness of earth. It is the radiance that shineth unto the perfect day. It is the bead that sparkles on the cup of immortality. It is the golden fruit that hangs on the tree of eternal life. Glorious thing is real virtue-based and wisdom-crowned affection. Earth without it would be colder than the icy grave. Heaven without it would be the deepest hell. So deep is the affectionate portion of our nature, and so thoroughly does it transfuse itself through our whole being, that we may well regard it as worthy of our deepest and most devout study, and our best efforts for its cultivation. It is the business of our schools to cultivate our intellects. It is the business of life to cultivate the affections. If we would consult our own happiness, if we would consult our own usefulness, if we would consult the well-being of our fellows, we shall strive to cultivate properly the affectionate portion of our natures.

But the question may occur to some of my young friends, "How shall I cultivate my affections—what course shall I pursue to develop their internal strength and beauty, and to guard them from evil?" First of all, you should seek a knowledge of genuine mental worth—of real spiritual excellence; study for an acquaintance with that which alone is the true and sure basis of affection. You should learn to admire *goodness* for its own intrinsic merit—for its own kindredness with God; to look upon *virtue* as supremely excellent and lovely; to cherish the deepest and most sincere respect for the real adornments of the inner man; to revere with all your soul moral excellence, moral force, the energy of moral power. You should cherish so perpet ually, so earnestly, and so devotedly your respect for the good, the beautiful, the true in human character, that wherever you find them you shall feel yourself wedded to them—feel yourself drawn to them by a spiritual attraction.

The first and highest, and most perpetual study of your life should be, to develop within yourself an absolute and positive *reverence* for moral purity and power. You should teach your soul to loathe impurity; to abhor, with a deep and hearty disgust, all moral debasement; to shudder at the thought of doing evil, or of seeing it in others. There is no such thing as cultivating too deep an abhorrence of evil, or too high a respect and admiration for moral excellence. The very thought of wrong should be cast out of the mind, as its most deadly enemy; while the thoughts of goodness, purity, all moral loveliness, should be cherished as angel guests, which are building up within you a sure foundation for pure and permanent affections. There is nothing else that seems to me to be of so much importance, of such priceless value, as a just appreciation of *moral worth.* It is not only the basis of all true affection, but the foundation of all that is noble, great, and good in human character. The basis of moral excellence may be placed in the religious principle. This is the only safe and sure foundation. The religious feelings, religious affections, religious sentiments should be cultivated most assiduously. The fervor of religious feelings should transfuse itself through the whole being. Religion should be held as a sacred and heavenly thing. Religious feelings should be respected everywhere, and in every body. We should hold them so supremely sacred, as to feel that we have no power to outrage the religious sentiments or feelings of any human being. And we should feel that an affection based on such a respect for things sacred and good, must be pure and permanent.

If we cultivate such feelings, such a reverence for virtue and religion, for all the excellencies of moral worth, we shall build up within ourselves a beautiful and glorious foundation for all the affections that ever glow in the human heart, and erect the only standard by which to judge of the purity and exeellency of the affections of others. We should learn to believe that no affection is to be looked upon with perfect confidence, that is not thus based upon the high ground of moral and religious sanctity and truth. And we should also learn to have the utmost confidence in affections thus based upon the most elevated feelings of the human soul. This will give a moral and religious aspect to the affections. It will give them the highest sanctions of the soul. It will make them redolent with sanctity and heaven. It will make the heart feel that God smiles upon all its loves. No idea, no feeling, gives such power to the human heart as a sense of the approval of God. And no thought sanctifies the affections as that which feels His divine presence filling the soul with its spirit and power.

When such a state of mind is attained, a basis is formed for the noblest and purest affections which can glow in a human heart. They will be built upon moral worth, and be fixed on this as their object. They will be deep, taking hold upon the most sanctified and godlike powers of the human soul. They will be firm, being supported by the

9*

holiest sanctions of conscience. They will be enlightened, being directed by the sunlight of reason. They will be lasting, being built upon a sure foundation. Nothing is clearer to my mind than that affection should be subject to the will, and directed according to the dictates of reason and conscience. The fires of affection should never be permitted to kindle till reason and conscience have decided upon the worthiness of the object. And when they have given a favorable decision, no earthly considerations should be permitted to quench the flames of love in the heart. The happiness, the purity of soul, the moral cultivation arising from the exercise of pure and genuine affections, are never to be weighed against considerations of a sinister and worldly character. Nothing is holier, nothing is lovelier, nothing is happier, nothing is more godlike than the heart's offering upon its altar of love. And hence nothing should be permitted to pollute the sacred gift. It is a heavenly thing, and should be viewed and treated as such. We should look upon pure affection with something of that feeling which we have when we think of God, or His holy heaven. It should be viewed with reverence. It should be regarded as a holy emanation from the Divinity. We should no more speak or think lightly of it than we would of the name of the most Holy One. We should no more make it a subject of wit, merriment, and laughter, than we would the most sacred rite of our holy religion. Any thing which is calculated to detract from the sacredness of the heart's affections, we should regard as a species of blasphemy. I have had my feelings as much and as often shocked at the light and contemptuous manner in which I have heard the heart's most sacred affections spoken of, as at the profanity and blasphemy that I have heard upon the street. All such remarks are truly painful to me, and it seems to me they must be to all who truly estimate the sacredness and loveliness of our affectionate natures. We can not expect to cultivate very much our affections till we have learned to respect and revere the heart, till it becomes to us a sacred, God-honored thing. When we have thus learned to respect all the affections of the heart, we have made much progress in the way of their cultivation. If we thus respect them, we shall use them tenderly and sacredly, use them much, and with great care, with respect to their object. And this leads me to the great means in the cultivation of the affections. It is their *use*—their *action*—directed by an enlightened judgment toward proper objects. It is the part of the judgment to choose the objects upon which our hearts shall fix their glowing energies. It is the part of the affections to love those objects with fervency and faithfulness; and in the exercise of their powers of attachment, they will acquire strength, permanency, purity, beauty, and energy. Every action augments their power, deepens their fervency, and extends their influence over the other powers and into the life. Every exercise enlarges their capacities, and makes more sublime and happy the soul in which they dwell. But there are various kinds of affection, each of which should be duly and properly cultivated.

I. First, is the affection which the young owe to their parents. And how strong and how pure it should be?

How can children ever half repay their parents for their watchings, anxieties, labors, toils, trials, patience, and love? Think of the utter helplessness of the long years of infancy, of the entire dependence of succeeding childhood, of the necessities and wants of youth, of the burning solicitude of parents, and their deep and inexhaustible love. Think of their long years of unwearied toil, of their deep and soul-felt devotion to the interests of their offspring, of the majesty and matchless power of their unselfish affections, and then say whether it is possible for youth to repay too much love and gratitude for all this bestowal of parental anxiety? Oh, what thankfulness should fill every youth's heart, what a glorious return of love! Every day should they make glad their parents' hearts. Every day should they give them some token of love. Every hour should their own hearts glow with gratitude and holy respect for those who have given them being, and loved them so fervently and long. Nothing is better to warm and quicken all the affections than such respect. Who can trust an ungrateful child? Who can believe that his affections for any object can be firm and pure? The child who has loved long and well his parents has thoroughly electrified his affections, has surcharged them with the sweet spirit of an affectionate tenderness, which will pervade his entire heart, and will make him better and holier forever. The affections of such a child are always to be trusted. As well may we doubt an angel, as such an one. And here let me say to all youth, in choosing your companions, those to whom you are to intrust your heart's treasures, choose those, and those only, who love well their parents. Such will be true as steel and tender as a mother's heart.

II. The *fraternal* is another kind of affection, which should be assiduously cultivated; that affection which exists between brothers and sisters of the same family. It is a beautiful and lovely feeling, and seems to me to be wholly unselfish, and angelic in its character. It must necessarily be a pure spiritual love. It arises not from a sense of gratitude, or for favors received, or from any thing else, but the endearing relationship of family. It rests not on any thing but a spiritual affinity of soul. It should be cultivated as one of the sweetest plants in the garden of the heart. It should be watered every morning and evening with the dews of good-nature, and sunned all day with the light of kindness. It should bear nothing but loving and tender words, even the dulcet music of home, see nothing but smiles and the tokens of confidence and sympathy, and know nothing but its own spirit of tenderness and unity. Home is the nursery of affection. It is love's cradling-place. It is the Eden of young attachments. And here should be planted and tended all the germs of love, every seed that shall ever sprout in the heart. And how carefully should they be tended; how guarded against the frosts of jealousy, anger, envy, pride, vanity, and ambition! How rooted in the best soil of the heart, and nourished and cultivated by the soul's best husbandry. If any would have fervent and noble affections, such as give power and glory to the human heart, such as sanctify the soul, and make it supremely beautiful, such as an angel might covet without shame, let him cultivate well all the *home feelings*, all that make *home* the most lovely place on earth, the only fit archetype of heaven. Home is the heart's garden. Its sunshine and its flowers are here. All its beautiful, all its lovely things are here. And here should be expended care, toil, effort, patience, and whatever may be necessary to make them still more lovely. We can not honor with too deep a reverence the home affections. We can not cultivate them with too assiduous a care. We can not cherish them with too much solicitude. For here is the center of our purest happiness, the spring of our deepest and strongest tides of joy.

When the home affections are duly cultivated, all others follow, or grow out of these, as a natural consequence. Home is the great seeding-place of every affection that ever grows in the heart. Hence I would say to all youth, to all children, to all parents, to all people, tend well the hearthstone garden. Watch, prune, and cultivate it with all prudence and wisdom, with all fervency of spirit. Let the music of the heart swell its notes here in one perpetual anthem of good-will. Let praise and prayer, and fervent good wishes, and words and works, hallow its sacred shrine. Let offices of love go round like smiles at a feast of joy. Let the whole soul devote its energies to making happy its home, and greatly will it be blessed, and greatly will it be honored.

III. Another affection which should be faithfully fostered is the *love of country*. Out of the love of home grows the wider love of country. This is a noble and generous affection. Patriotism is a holy altar-fire of the human soul.

In a country like ours there is every possible inducement to give it its highest and purest expression. If the Laplander, chilling among his banks of eternal snow; or the Russian, ground by the hand of oppression; or the Turk, forced to be a tool of power, lust, and caprice; or the Chi nean, shut out from the world, and in his den, where ignorant hordes are born and die in poverty and stupidity, can shout, and fight, and die for his country, what ought not the American youth to feel and do! Talk of other lands! England's glory, as queen of the seas; France, with her hills of grape and her groves of pleasure; Italy, with her sunny skies, her genial clime, and monuments of other days of grandeur! What are they, compared to our own great land of prairie and sloping hill, of broad rivers and rolling lakes; of wide savannas; of continents of corn, and wheat, and cotton; of cane, and grass, and grazing herds; of towns, and cities, and states; of busy millions of free, happy, thriving people, with schools, colleges, and churches at their doors; and telegraphs, railroads, and libraries in all their towns? What are they, huddled and cramped in their crowded little corners, jostling against each other at every turn, compared with our broad sweep of territory stretching from sunrise to sunset, the unbroken solitudes of which would hide the European millions from the light of the sun and sight of the world? We have room to strive, and labor, and grow, and enough to grow on. If ever youth had the stimulus of all things great and glorious, to awaken their patriotism and stir their young blood in their country's behalf, the youth of America must be the favored ones. Liberty's home, freedom's cradle, religion's altar, humanity's shrine, learning's retreat, the ark of safety and the olive branch of peace are all theirs. Every thing that can be afforded by outward advantages, that the Creator can give or the government bestow, are laid in profuse abundance at their feet. They have but to step into the field, and saw, and pluck, and eat; they have but to do their duty to be honored, enriched, and blessed with all needed worldly comforts and spiritual opportunities and excellences.

Love their country! They are the most ungrateful children in the world if they do not. Such ingratitude would show them unworthy of their country's blessings; unworthy the sires whose names they bear, or the noble mothers who bore them. The very literature of our country is like the shining heavens for beauty. It is studded with names which are blazing suns in the moral firmament, and glittering with deeds and lives of glory that have come upon the world like a quick fall of stars. Our sciences are as solid as our literature is beautiful; and our mechanism as useful as our land is free. Who can fail to love such a country? A country's hope and promise are its youth; and when a country does every thing for its youth, they, in turn, ought to do much for her, at least love her with pure hearts fervently, and serve her with clean hand and noble lives honorably.

Patriotism is shown in deeds, in lives which do honor to a country, and strengthen the pillars of moral principle on which she rests. Let American youth vie with each other in making strong the right arm of their country's virtue and honor, and in laying deep in their hearts the principles of her permanency and prosperity.

IV. Out of a true love of country should grow a wider one, one which should reach round the world, one which should encompass the race. On the soil of America and in the hearts of her youth should philanthropy rear her asylum for the oppressed of all nations. The genuine spirit of reform and progress should be cradled in the bosom of every son and daughter of our home of the free and the brave. The watchword of every youth should be "Excelsior"—onward and upward—not for himself alone, but for the world. The world his large heart should love; the world he should honor with his wishes, prayers, and affections. Man is everywhere brother to his fellow. Fraternity is the girdle of nations. The race is one. It is a family of God. Where may we look with more confidence for the embodiment of this grand feeling of fraternity than to the hearts and lives of American youth? True reform grows out of fraternal affection, the principle of philanthropy. Every American should be a genuine reformer; not a hunter after something *new*, but a hunter after something *good;* something that will bless men everywhere; something as universal in its application and utility as the principle of political and religious liberty, which we offer as our gift-example to the world. Not content should we be till our blessings encircle and illumine the whole earth. In the cause of human redemption should we labor, as self-consecrated missionaries, loving and blessing wherever we go.

Thus do we and may we cultivate the noble affections which the Father has given us, enlarging and ennobling our own hearts, blessing and making happy our fellows from our home outward through parents, brothers, sisters, companions, friends, and country, till we at length reach our arms around our race and fold it to our bosom, as the great family which it is our duty and privilege to love and bless.

LECTURE XIV.

COURTSHIP.

The Season of Courtship the most Important part of Life—Too Serious a Matter for a Joke—Why Marriage is a Lottery—Superficial Courtship—Marriage Reveals the True Character—Love Character, not Person merely—Feeling, not Reason, leads astray—True Object of Courtship—Proper Age to Select Companions—Childish Courtships unsafe—Evils of Premature Marriages—False Ideas of Married Life—Proper Age to Marry—A Companion without a Character—What is a Companion?—Courtship should Reveal the True Character—Mutual Hypocrisy and Deception—Court for the Future as well as for the Present—True Marriage not a Lottery.

What! a lecture on courtship! methinks my reader exclaims. Yes; why not? Is not courtship an important matter; and is not the period of courtship an important part of every one's life? Is it not important to know how to court well, as well as to know how to do any thing else well? Bad courting is the worst business in the world; and a poor job at it results in the most horrid consequences. Conjugal infelicity is earth's most fiery hell. It is occasioned by bad courting. Young reader, if you wish to live peacefully and pleasantly with your companion, and set the world an example of a true life, come and sit down with me, and let us learn how to court. Come with a serious soul, with an earnest desire to be benefited. Lay aside lightness and jesting. Joke about courting! As well may you joke about the most solemn realities of religion, death, and eternity. It is one of the most serious matters of life. Your weal or woe, and the weal or woe of those that shall come after you, and the influence you shall exert upon the world, depend in a great manner upon the wisdom and virtue with which you conduct your preparation for marriage. Joke about such a matter! It is a horrid outrage upon the most holy and exalted feelings of the human soul, and the most sacred and important relation of life. It is a vulgarism and wickedness to be compared only to blasphemy. It had, and still has, its origin in the basest lust. The refined soul is always disgusted with it. It is awfully demoralizing in its tendency, and low and base in its character. It is true, many bandy their low jokes upon this matter in thoughtlessness. But if they would take one moment's sober reflection upon it, they would see the impropriety of jesting about the most delicate, serious, and sacred feelings and relations in human existence. The whole tendency of such lightness is to cause the marriage relation to be lightly esteemed, and courtship to be made a round of low fun and frolic, in which every species of deception is endeavored to be played off. Until it is viewed in its true light, in that sober earnestness which the subject demands, how can courtship be any thing else than a grand game of hypocrisy, resulting in wickedness and misery the most ruinous and deplorable?

Listen to the jests on this subject in every gay circle among the old and young. Do they not all clearly show that their authors regard courtship as a grand cheat—a game of chance, in which the most skillful in deception is the winner; and do they not, by the expression of such debasing views, encourage this wooing fraud among the young? Nothing in the common practice of men is more deleterious in its consequences than the light, frivolous manner in which courtship and marriage are treated. They are made the subjects of the lowest and rudest nonsense and vulgarity. And almost the whole community seem to enter into this tirade of practical slander against the highest proprieties of life and virtue. And by the gust of pleasure that seems to attend it, we should judge that it is enjoyed. A sad commentary is this upon the virtuous feeling of the community.

Let all joking, low vulgarities, innuendoes, hints, puns, and nonsense on this subject be most heartily disapproved; yea, condemned as absolutely wrong and baneful in their influence. Especially let the virtuous and pure-minded discountenance every thing of the kind by precept and example.

"Marriage is a lottery," exclaims almost every man and woman you meet. And why is it so? Simply because courtship is a grand scheme of deception. Is it not so? Who courts *honestly?* Some, it is true; but few, indeed. Let us see; it is conducted something like this. A young man and woman meet at a party, ball, school, or church. The young man sees something in the lady that attracts his attention; it may be her pretty face, her golden curls, her flashing eyes, her delicate hand or slender waist, or snowy neck, or graceful carriage, or more likely, the *plumage* in which the bird shines. He looks again, and then again, and without one particle of sense or reason for it, save that he has caught the fair one's eye, his attraction rises into captivation. He seeks an introduction. A little parly of nonsense ensues, about fashions, parties, beaux and belles, and a few jokes pass about "invitations," "captivations," "runaway matches," etc.; then an appointment for another meeting, a walk, a visit to a saloon, a neighbor, or something of the kind, follows, and they part, both determined, in the utmost desperation, to catch the prize, if possible. They dream, and sing, and make verses about each other, and meditate ways and means to appear captivating at the next meeting, till it arrives; when, lo! they meet, all wreathed in smiles, and shining in beautiful things. How can it be otherwise than that their captivation shall became absolute adoration now. The afternoon and evening are spent together, each in perfect delight. They talk about flowers, and stars, and poetry; and give hints, and signs, and tokens, till each understands the other's captivation. They part, with an engagement to meet again. Now comes the tug of war. How shall they keep up the captivation? Every device is resorted to; smiles are profuse, deceits in standing, business, wealth, associates, character, dispositions, opinions, tastes, education, and almost every thing else are now practiced; not with a view particularly to deceive, but to please. Thus passes away a month or two, or three, perhaps, in sunshine warm and fresh as ever shone, and the happy pair are married; full of the most visionary expectations of happiness, and ardent and sincere in their affections as human hearts can well be. They know nothing of each other's *real* characters. They are acquainted only with their courtship characters. They do not love each other's real characters, for they know not what they are; but their courtship characters they love with all their souls. And why should they not; they were beautiful and pleasing; full of tenderness, self-sacrifice, ardor, and affection. No one can help loving such characters, and the persons that bear them.

Married life now comes, and ushers in its morning glory, and they are happy as a happy pair can well be, for a while. But "life is real," and character is real, and love is real. When life's *reality* comes, they find things in each other's characters that perfectly startle them. Every day reveals something new and something unpleasant. The courtship character slowly fades away, and with it the courtship love. Now comes disappointment, sorrow, regret. They find that their characters are entirely dissimilar. Married life is a burden, full of cares, vexations, and disappointments. But they must make the best of it, and BEAR *it through.* Yes, marriage is a lottery. They know it. Some may get prizes, and some may not. No one knows before he draws, whether he will draw a blank or a prize. This is their conclusion.

Now, is it not just and right that they should be miserable? They acted like fools, and they have no right to complain at the just and natural consequences of their senseless course. It is right to love, and love earnestly, but they *should* have known what they loved. They should have loved in the light, and not in the dark; should have loved by wisdom, and not by impulse; should have *known* what they loved, and not love an imaginary character. They went about it as though it was a mere childish work of fancy, and not as about a solemn, life-lasting reality. They meant well, but they did not *think* well and *act* well. Their intentions were good, but their actions were very unwise.

In the first place, they had no right "to fall in love at first sight." They might have been pleased and interested in each other at once; but they should have known how and why they were interested, should have understood the secret of that interest, and been sure that it was an interest founded in the *spiritual character*, and not in the outward person or dress, form or feature. It is *character* that we love, and not *person*. We invest every person we love with a character, and we love him or her for that character, and not for the person. The most pleasing person in the world becomes disgusting when known to possess a bad character; and the most unpleasant personal figure becomes interesting when known to be the habitation of an angelic soul. Now, how can love at first sight be any thing else than a love of the *person?* A *character* can not be known so quick. Such a love is not to be trusted. It is unwise, and rests upon no firmer foundation than fancy, or something worse. It has no guarentee of continuance, and should not be relied upon as of any value, not even as a seed for a riper and fuller love. "Love at first sight" is generally a vision of the fancy, originating in a fevered or morbid state of mind. It is a mere "will-of-the-wisp," that will do well enough to look at, if we never mind any thing about it. It is sometimes the case that highly congenial characters impress each other with a conviction of their congeniality at their first meeting, which conviction arises from the absolute evidences of character, and not from visions of beauty floating about the person. As long as people marry from "love at first sight," we must expect that they will believe that marriage is a lottery, and that they have drawn a blank.

In the second place, they did not court in the right way. They courted by impulse, and not by judgment; it was a process of wooing, and not of discovery; it was an effort to please, and not a search for companionship; it was done with excitement, and not with calmness and deliberation; it was done in haste, and not with cautious prudence; it was a vision of the heart, and not a solemn reality; it was conducted by feeling, and not by reason; it was so managed as to be a perpetual blandishment of pleasure the most intoxicating and delightful, and not a trying ordeal for the enduring realities of solid and stubborn life; it was a perpetual yielding up of every thing, and not a firm maintaining of every thing that belongs to the man or woman. In almost every particular it was false, and hence must be followed by evil consequences. All similar courting is bad, absolutely wrong.

I. Courting is not *children's play*. Nothing is further from right than children's wooing. Boys and girls should love each other's society, and should enjoy it as much as possible. They should be reared together, and educated together, even through their entire course of study. A girl should never be sent to school where there are no boys, and a boy where there are no girls. The softening, subduing, moralizing, and stimulating influence of each sex should be felt upon the other. It is very great, and an influence which can not well be dispensed with in the proper training of the young character. But their intercourse should be the intercourse of young friends. Marriage is a subject of too deep importance for them to think of, only as a most important step, to be taken when age and experience shall have given them sufficient wisdom to take it with discretion. Their social intercourse should be general, and not particular. They should study each other's happiness, and enjoy much each other's society. And their intercourse should be courteous, refined, prudent, and obliging. The young gentleman and the young lady should be fully developed in early youth. They should study to be graceful, courteous, free and easy in each other's society. Every thing that is coarse, inelegant, and unchaste in word and action should be studiously avoided. Rudeness, wildness, boisterous conversation, loud laughing, coarse jokes, and every thing kindred with these things are out of place in the society of young gentleman and ladies, and when they are indulged in or permitted without rebuke they show a degree of ill-breeding and want of refinement greatly to be disapproved and regretted.

But not in childhood should any youth think of choosing a companion. The ostensible object of courtship is the choice of a companion. For no other object should any intercourse having the appearance of courtship be permitted or indulged in. It is a species of high-handed fraud upon an unsuspecting heart, worthy of the heaviest penalty of public opinion, or law. The affections are too tender and sacred to be trifled with. He who does it is a wretch. He should be ranked among thieves, robbers, villains, and murderers. He who steals money steals trash; but he who steals affections without a return of similar affections, steals that which is dearer than life and more precious than wealth. His theft is a robbery of the heart.

There is much trifling courting among the young in some portions of the country, that results in such calamitous consequences; carried on sometimes when the young man means nothing but present pleasure, and sometimes when the young woman has no other object in view. Such intercourse is confined mostly to young men and women before they are of age. It is a crying evil, worthy of the severest censure. The mothers of all such youth should know when they are out. This evil has its origin chiefly in the haste to get married, so strongly evinced by many young persons, even before they are of age. How are children, or youth, not of age, capable of choosing companions for life, such as shall render their married life their greatest earthly blessing, as it should? The law regards them as incapable of taking care of themselves, of making civil contracts, because of their want of wisdom. How then can they be capable of contracting for a companion for life? and forming a contract, too, requiring as much wisdom, insight into character, knowledge of human nature, and as great a use of real judgment, as any act we have to perform in our whole life?

Nothing is more preposterous, absurd, and dangerous than childhood courting. It is almost sure to result in disappointment, anguish, remorse, or a hap-hazard marriage. All such early marriage alliances are hap-hazard alliances and the resultant marriages are lotteries. Childhood marriages are lotteries. This fact is incontrovertable. No girl under eighteen or boy under twenty-one is capable of choosing a companion with any degree of certainty, which will be such as they shall want in all the stern realities of life. Those who will madly risk the choice so early, must risk the consequences, and not complain when the evil day cometh. Because I fancy a girl at sixteen for a wife, is no good reason why I should fancy her at twenty-five. Her character at sixteen is not formed. She does not know herself what she will be at twenty-five, nor does her mother, or any human being. That character depends upon the hidden forces of her soul, which none can detect but the most skillful reader of the scientific language of psychology and upon the circumstances which shall attend her life And equally undeveloped is a young man's character at nineteen. Who can tell what he will be? The girl that gives her life into his keeping at that age, is mad with folly or drunk with the intoxication of childish passion. And the young man and woman who form a solemn matrimonial alliance at that age, or any age before they have attained manhood and womanhood, do it more in folly than in wisdom, more in passion than in love, do it at the risk of their life's peace, and the most fearful consequences that follow in the train of such matrimonial adventures. It can only be called a matrimonial adventure. They do it in childish ignorance. It is not possible for a youth at that age to have a judgment sufficiently matured, and a heart sufficiently subdued, to render him capable of forming an absolutely correct opinion upon a subject of such vast importance and such complicated results. Treat it lightly as you will, it is a subject of the most momentous importance to human virtue, prosperity, and happiness, and involves much of the most intricate and profound philosophy of human life, conduct, and character. Give a subject like this into the hands of children, and we must expect such crazy consequences as we see almost everywhere prevailing; and we may expect that they will in life come to the conclusion that marriage is a lottery, an opinion as far from being a necessary truth as it is wicked in its influence. I grant that marriage is a lottery with many, and with all who marry very young; but it should be with none.

A subject of such vast importance requires the matured powers of manhood and womanhood, and the experience and observation of such maturity.

My observation has taught me that very early marriages are very seldom eminently prosperous and happy. The burning passion in which they were consummated soon cools, and is succeeded by indifference; giving a seeming proof of that common saying, that "hot love is soon cold," a lie on its face, which has grown out of the exhibitions of early passion.

There is a vast difference between passion and love. Passion is of the animal, and fleeting; love is of the angel, and enduring. That which they fancy is love in their silly courtships soon passes away in the reality and freedom of marriage, and is succeeded by a sort of childish indifference, in which the companion is regarded something in the light of any family member, and treated as though they had grown up together, and might find fault with each other, and speak of and to each other as though all thought of the sacred relation existing between them had been forgotten. Nearly all persons early married, with whom I have been acquainted, give me, in a few years after the marriage, the impression that their nuptial day, and all its tenderness, and all the refined, delicate feelings and memories that have their birth in that hour, have been forgotten, or are remembered only to laugh over; while individuals married in mature age carry with them through life the memories of their union, and the conviction of the importance, blessedness, and holiness of the state into which it ushered them, as the sweetest and most cherished recollections treasured in their minds. I believe this difference is not fanciful, but real. It grows out of the fact that early marriages are premature, and never properly understood or appreciated. When this is the case, marriage soon comes to be viewed as a commonplace matter, and results in no real happiness, no sacred joy, no high, virtuous influence, no holy, consecrated life. Very early marriages are generally unions of persons, and not unions of spirits; they are outward, and not inward unions.

Such marriages, then, are hazardous in the extreme, and

f.r many reasons are generally wrong. A lady should seldom be married under twenty-two and a gentleman under twenty-four. A marriage consummated before twenty-five, with a lady, and before twenty-seven, with a gentleman, is an early marriage. And they can not well be prepared to marry intellectually or physically before these periods. Very early marriages have been contended for only on the ground that marriage is a lottery, and a bad draw could be got along better when the mind was very young and pliant, so as to be bent to any thing, than after it had acquired a fixed character. Only think of it, a companion without a fixed character! A baby husband or wife! The thought is ridiculous. Character should be fixed before marriage, and none should be united but such as are congenial and adapted to each other. Any *man* or *woman* would despise a companion without a character. The *character* is the thing we marry as much as the person. It is the character we admire, the character we love, the character we are influenced by, the character that is to bless us in the married state, the character that is to direct our family, and give standing, respect, and tone, to our household. Characters are not well enough fixed to be absolutely certain, till manhood and womanhood are fully attained.

II. I have remarked that the ostensible object of courtship is the choice of a companion. It is not to woo; it is not to charm or gratify, or please, simply for the present pleasure; it is not for the present sweets of such an intimate and confiding intercourse. It is simply and plainly for the selection of a life's companion—one who must bear, suffer, and enjoy life with us, in all its frowns and smiles, joys and sorrows—one who can walk pleasantly, willingly, and confidingly, by our side, through all the intricate and changing vicissitudes incident to mortal life. Now, how shall courtship be conducted, so as to make marriage a *certainty* and not a lottery? This is the question.

Now let us ask, what is to be sought? You answer, a companion. What is a companion? A congenial spirit, one possessed of an interior constitution of soul similar to our own, of similar age, opinions, tastes, habits, modes of thought, and feeling. A congenial spirit is one who, under any given combination of circumstances, would be affected, and feel and act as we ourselves would. It is one who would enjoy what we would enjoy, dislike what we would dislike, approve what we would approve, and condemn what we would condemn, not for the purpose of agreeing with us, but of his or her own free will. This is a companion; one who is kindred in soul with us; who is already united to us by the ties of spiritual harmony; which union it is the object of courtship to discover. Courtship, then, is a voyage of discovery; or a court of inquiry, established by mutual consent of the parties, to see wherein and to what extent there is a harmony existing between their spiritual beings. It is not for the purpose of effecting a harmony, or of forcing a union, or of coaxing one, but simply to see whether one exists already.

Unions are formed by God himself in the spiritual beings. These unions are to be found. When a young man and woman meet, and form an acquaintance, if they imagine, from the pleasure they feel in each other's society, from expressed opinions, from known or supposed character, from personal appearance, or any thing else, that there is a true spiritual harmony existing between them, it is their duty as well as a privilege to establish a court of inquiry, or courtship, as the world calls it, for the purpose of comparing their souls or their real characters; to see wherein and to what extent they are harmonious; to see how much they are alike and how much they are unlike; to see whether they are companions in heart or not. This, when faithfully performed, is not always the most pleasant inquiry in the world. It is often a severe ordeal, requiring great self-denial and sacrifice. To unvail one's soul to the gaze of another, and that other the one of all the world whom we wish to have respect us most—to expose to the full blaze of light our inmost characters, our faults, our weaknesses, our passions, our most exposed points—to tell how easily we are tempted, how readily we yield to evil circumstances, and how conscious we are of our own want of moral strength and true harmony of soul, is not a pleasant task; and yet it is a task which should be faithfully performed. All these weaknesses and inharmonies must be revealed in the married state; they can not then be long concealed. That is a state of freedom, of the most perfect exposure. The most indescribable shades and tints of character will be revealed in it. If you conceal yourself in courtship, you can not always do it. Believe it, marriage is a state of spiritual exposure; courtship should be

10*

its proper forerunner. What we are to give and what we are to get, should be known before we enter into indissoluble bonds. A failure to seek and impart this knowledge has caused untold anguish and mortification.

Courtship, as it is generally conducted, is a game at "blindman's buff," only that both parties are blinded. They voluntarily blind themselves, and then blind each other; and thus they "go it blind," till their eyes are opened in marriage. But not faults alone should be revealed and studied, but the whole character. It is emphatically a study; a study of character, of soul, the most intricate and difficult in the world. It should be commenced with a careful and faithful expression and comparison of opinions. Every opinion entertained by either party upon every subject of interest, should be carefully expressed and compared with the other's opinion on the same subject. I do not mean discussion of opinion, but comparison. Nor should it be a hasty comparison, but a long and thorough one, revealing the exact point of view in which every subject is viewed, the amount and kind of information had upon the subject, and the degree and color of light in which an opinion has been formed. Opinions are among the best indices of character. Hence, this comparison of opinion should be most thorough. If there is not a general harmony of opinion, the subject should be discussed and the court adjourned forever. The parties should not be satisfied with a partial agreement, or a half-way harmony, and dismiss the subject with an agreement to disagree. Every one may rest assured that this agreement will be broken, or at least it will always be a source of disquietude, anxiety, and regret. When opinions are not harmonious they can only result in unhappiness.

First and most important of all opinions are the *religious*. On a subject so important and so dear as religion, there must be a harmony, or, to say the least, there will be a very great loss of pleasure, a continued and deep anxiety in both minds, and much secret unhappiness. It is impossible that it should be otherwise. And hence this subject should be earnestly and prayerfully considered. It matters not whether the parties have made an open profession of any religious sentiment or not. Every body of any worth has religious opinions and biases. Then opinions on the various subjects of reform, of philanthropy, life, and duty, should have their due share of attention; the subjects of education, the best modes of instruction, the best influences in a family, the kind of family government, and all the subjects that will ever interest a growing family; among which will come expenses, manner of living, dress, equipage, taste, visiting, traveling, reading, industry, econ omy, tattling, gossip, expectations, desires, objects of life, marriage, money, honor, etc. If in all these things there is found to be a general harmony of opinion, the parties may descend to more minute particulars, may go into the sacred sanctuary of the affections, and talk of the feelings, the tender impulses, and of the manner in which they desire to live, in the conjugal relation; going out into every subject that is in any manner to effect their happiness, in the most secret and retired relations of the state of perfect physical and spiritual intimacy they are contemplating. If in all these they honestly and inmostly agree, and find a deep and thrilling pleasure in their agreement, find their union of sentiment to give a charm to their social intercourse; if now they feel that their hearts are bound as well as their sentiments in a holy unity, and that for each other they would live, and labor, and make every personal sacrifice with gladness, and that without each other they know not how to live, it is their privilege, yes, their *duty*, to form a matrimonial alliance. And it will not be a lottery. They know what they are to give and what they are to get. They will be married in the full blaze of light and love; and be married for a happy, virtuous, and useful union, to bless themselves and the world with a living type of heaven.

LECTURE XV.

MARRIAGE

Marriage, the Foundation of the Social Fabric—Improper Marriage a living Misery—Marriage should be made a Study—Ignorance, the Bane of Matrimony—Importance of the Results of Marriage—Characteristics of the Sexes—Contrasts and Affinities of Character—Goodness does not constitute Harmony—Duty of nearly all to Marry—Matrimonial Candidates Classified—A true Mate the other half of Self—Honesty in Matrimonial Matters—Marrying for a Home, Money, or Passion—Study thy Constitution—Harmony of Temperament—Intellectual Adaptation—Moral and Social Harmony—A thorough Acquaintance necessary.

Of all the institutions that affect human weal or woe in the earth, none is more important than Marriage. It is the foundation of the great social fabric; and conceals within its mystic relations the coiled secret of the largest proportion of happiness and misery connected with the sublunary lot of mortals.

When God formed man, He said, "It is not good for him to be alone." So He says of each man and each woman now, "It is not good for him or her to be alone." This is the Divine annunciation written in the social constitution of the race. Not in the Bible only, but in the heart of every man and woman, it is found. A marriage-altar is erected in every soul by the Hand that made us; and at that altar the Divinity presides, solemnizing, in a covenant of eternal beauty, peace, and love, the marriage of its rightful partner. It is true that God marries the truly married. He joins the spirit partners; and what He joins no man can put asunder. Their persons may be separated, and forced into other relations, but their spirits remain locked in the eternal embraces of a divinely-appointed union.

All the blessedness, all the utility, efficacy, and happiness of the married state, depends upon its truthfulness, or the wisdom of the union. Marriage is not necessarily a blessing. It may be the bitterest curse. It may sting like an adder and bite like a serpent. Its bower is as often made of thorns as of roses. It blasts as many sunny expectations as it realizes. Every improper marriage is a living misery, an undying death. Its bonds are grated bars of frozen iron. It is a spirit prison, cold as the dungeon of ruin. An illy-mated human pair is the most woeful picture of human wretchedness that is presented in the book of life; and yet, such pictures are plenty. Every page we turn gives us a view of some such living bondage. But a proper marriage, a true interior, soul-linked union is a living picture of blessedness, unrivaled in beauty. A true marriage is the soul's Eden. It is the portal of heaven. It is the visiting-place of angels. It is the charm indescribable of a spirit in captivation with all imaginable beauty and loveliness. It is a constant peace-offering, that procures a continual Sabbath-day sweetness, rich as the quietude of reposing angels. It is not given to words to express the refinement of pleasure, the delicacy of joy, and the abounding fullness of satisfaction, that those feel whom God hath joined in a high marriage of spirit. Such a union is the highest schcol of virtue, the soul's convent, where the ves tal fires of purity are kept continually burning.

Marriage, then, to be a blessing must be properly entered. It has its fundamental laws, which must be obeyed. Like every good institution, it is subject to fixed and invariable laws; and all its blessings are obtained by conformity to these laws. Marriage is not a mysterious wonder-working institute of the Almighty, which can not be studied by the common mind, but a simple necessity laid in man's social nature, which may be read and understood of all men who will investigate that nature. The reasons for every enjoyment of the matrimonial life may be understood before entering upon its relations. The conditions upon which its joys and advantages are realized may be learned before hand. It should not be entered in blindness, but rather in the daylight of a perfect knowledge of its rules and regulations, its provisions and conditions, its laws and privileges, so that no uncertainty shall attend its realization, no unhappy revealments shall follow a knowledge of its reality.

Marriage, then, should be made a study. Every youth, both male and female, should so consider it. It is the grand social institution of humanity. Its laws and relations are of momentous importance to the race. Shall it be entered blindly, in total ignorance of what it is, what its conditions of happiness are? Its relations involve some of the most stern duties and acts of self-denial that men are called upon to perform. Shall youth enter upon such relations without a knowledge of these duties? If they do, they must expect unhappy consequences. How unwise would be that man who should assume the responsibilities of a pilot upon one of our rivers, without any previous study either of the river or business. What folly would he exhibit who should attempt the duties of an engineer on a railroad or steamboat, in total ignorance of the nicely adjusted and powerful machinery placed under his control. What foolhardiness would he exhibit, who, in entire ignorance of the human system, should attempt to perform a critical surgical operation. And how perfectly irrational would she appear who should assume the position of a teacher of the higher sciences and accomplishments of elegant life, without any previous preparation or study. And yet, not more inconsistent would be these several courses of conduct, than his or hers who enters, unprepared by previous study and forethought, upon the earnest realities of married life. For all the professions, trades, and callings in life men and women prepare themselves by previous attention to their principles and duties. They study them; devote time, and money, and toil to them. Every imaginable case of difficulty or trial is considered and duly disposed of according to the general principles of the trade or profession. But marriage, incomparably the most important and holy relation of life, involving the most sacred responsibilities and influences, social, civil, and religious, that bear upon men, is entered upon in hot haste, or blind stupidity, by a great majority of youth. How few make this great social relation a serious study, inquiring into all its regulations and seeking useful information concerning all its blissful privileges and the duties growing out of them. No subject should be more seriously contemplated by youth than this. The nature, and character, and wonderful mystery and beauty of the sexual relation should be most carefully and studiously investigated. The entire object of this relation, both in its physical and spiritual aspects, as involving the reproduction of the Divine image in generation after generation, increasing beyond all human computation the field of sentience and moral accountability, of life, activity, progress, and spiritual glory, and uniting in the bonds of a universal relationship the vast family of man, binding them all in the silken ties of a spiritual affinity, which are the sources of universal love, and out of which grow the common duties of fraternity, which are so delightful to contemplate and glorious to realize, should be studied as the grand science of life and love. It should be studied as a source of wisdom, a means of virtue, and a fountain of love. The singular beauty and adaptedness of this relation to men in this world, is so apparent and wonderful, that no one can see and appreciate it without a feeling of gratitude to its Divine Author and Giver. It has been said that an "undevout astronomer is mad." With much more propriety might it be said, that a student of this beautiful and marvelous relation is mad. The starry heavens is a scene of cold, shining, physical grandeur; but this relation enshrines an ardent, soul-bearing love, as rich in rational charms and enduring virtue as it is glorious in its intellectual and moral results. Then let every youth study this entire subject in all its bearings and relations with devout and serious earnestness. The physical and mental constitution of the two sexes come most ligitimately within the sphere of this study. The duties that belong to each, the privileges that each may expect at the hands of the other, the respect and tenderness due from each to the other, and the constant watchfulness over and interest in each other that they should always feel, without one moment's cessation, which ought to grow out of the sexual relation, and always will if it is not abused, are most proper topics of reflection as connected with this subject.

No young man has any right to ask a young woman to enter the matrimonial bonds with him, till he is thoroughly acquainted with the female constitution and character. How can he be to her that guardian, friend, and companion, which he should be, if he knows not the delicacy of her physical make, the laws to which it is subject, the gentle treatment it requires, and the sensitiveness of her feelings, the objects of her strongest respect, and the sources of her most refined pleasures. Woman is so constituted that she can *bear* almost every thing, and still live on, and feel that her best feelings must be martyrs to her husband's coarseness or ignorance; but at the same time she has capacities for the most pure and lofty enjoyments, for refined pleasures, for exquisite delicacies of sentiment and feeling, which her husband should be able fully to gratify. This he can always do if he is properly acquainted with her nature. Woman loves the strong, the resolute, and the vigorous in man. To these qualities she looks for protection. Under the shadow of their wings she feels secure. Bu she wants them blended with the tender, the sensitive, and the lofty in sentiment. Her companionship, her joy, she finds in these. It is in these that she meets her lover; to these she pours the full tides of her loving soul; and in response to these she enters the bower of conjugal felicity. He who knows not her nature, knows not how to gratify and satisfy that nature.

So woman should know the nature of man. The rough world often makes him appear what he is not. He has a vein of tenderness below the rocky strata of his worldly man, which woman should know how to penetrate and bring up for her own as well as his enjoyment. It is in this strata of tenderness that she finds her true companionship with him, and he with her. If she is ignorant of his nature, she knows not how to supply his wants or answer the calls of that nature. Their natures, though different, are singularly adapted to each other. When his is bold and hers is trembling, she flies in gladness to him for shelter. When his is strong and hers is weak, she trustingly leans on him for strength. When hers is warm and his is cold, he gladly and lovingly nestles in her bosom, to be warmed into the resistless charms of love. When hers is confiding and his reserved, he with a deep joy opens his heart to her confidence. Man has something peculiar to his character, which is the masculine element of humanity; woman possesses a peculiarity as marked, which is the feminine element of humanity. These two, though different, are not repulsive to each other, but strongly attractive. These peculiarities must be known, and known before mar riage, or there will be seasons of unhappiness in the conjugal state. It is ignorance in these matters that causes a great amount of matrimonial infelicity. Then this very ignorance renders both young men and women incapable of selecting a companion suitable to their own natures. A good man and a good woman will not always make each other a suitable companion. They may both be very excellent people, and be so different in many respects as to render them wholly unfit for each other.

Before we can select a companion for ourselves and do it intelligently, we must know what we want. To know this, we must know our own nature, our wants, just how we shall live and act in the married state; must know what we want a companion for, whether for work, for a home, for a drudge, for the gratification of passion, or for true companionship. Every youth should examine himself well, to see what views of life operate most strongly upon him in respect to a contemplated companionship. If they are not high and honorable, he may hope for but little real joy in the married state.

Thus we see most clearly the necessity of a thorough study of this whole subject by every youth. No one can make an enlightened choice of a companion without an enlightened view of the whole subject. I say *every* youth; for it is true that every youth should look forward to marriage as a duty which he ought to perform, not unwillingly, it is true, but gladly. The period of the latter youth should be considered and so lived as to be a meet preparation for matrimony.

The young man who marries not, except in a few exceptional cases arising out of ill-health, deformity, malformation, or great perversity of temper, or eccentricity of character, fails in one of the most palpable duties of life. He deprives himself of life's most refined and exalted pleasures, of some of its strongest incentives to virtue and activity, sets an example unworthy of imitation, and fails to do much good that he ought to do to society. Moreover, he leaves one who might have made him a happy and useful companion, to pine in maidenhood of heart through all the weary days of life, to be less useful to society than she might have been, had he performed his duty to himself and her. I would not make marriage the sole end of youth's thoughts and labors. They should prepare for a life of usefulness whether they marry or not. One may be very happy and very useful who never marries, if he lives for a worthy object in life. He or she who prepares in early youth for a true and useful life will be prepared for marriage. Marriage is real life, not a moonshine shadow. To prepare for it, is to prepare for just such a life as will be a blessing to the world. The silly theorist about marriage, the lovelorn whiner, the passion-burnt anchorist, the endless talker about its sweets and pleasures, and vague longer for its privilege, are making but a poor preparation for it. It wants sober study, solid life, earnest thought, high aims and noble purposes, to prepare for the proper performance of its exalted and pleasurable duties. Such should be the preparation of every youth. But let us consider some things necessary to an intelligent choice of a companion.

We have said that God marries the truly married. This no doubt is true. He sanctions the union of those fitted for each other. True unions are founded in congeniality of spirit. This is the fundamental law of marriage. There is a certain class of women, how large or how small, we pretend not to say, that are so nearly alike in their feelings, desires, aspirations, and spiritual characteristics, that they impress their most intimate friends in a most similar manner. There is also a certain class of men, so kindred in their natures, that when you know one you know them all, who, under similar circumstances, will always all be affected alike and act alike. Their spiritual constitutions are kindred; they are formed after the similitude of the same pattern. Call this class of men class A, and this class of women class A. Now any one of these women would make a suitable companion for any one of these men. And so of the men. Between these two classes there is a harmony, a congeniality, a kindredness, that would render them proper companions for each other. When any two of these are united, they are truly united. Their hearts flow together; their souls blend in one; their natures coalesce; their lives mingle like the meeting of two mountain streams, and flow sweetly on together. Intellectually, morally, socially, spiritually, they become one. Like the halves of the same golden globe, they meet and unite, and their union forms a sphere or circle in the spiritual realm, in which the harmony of existence is felt and manifested. A single individual is always but half an existence or unity. The race are formed in pairs. A pair constitutes a unit, or spiritual circle, capable of feeling and manifesting the harmony of being. A single being existing alone is always inharmonious, incomplete. Something is wanting to make it whole and perfect in the play and activity of its feelings. That something is its mate. That mate is kindred with itself, the other half of itself. They think, feel, and act as one when united. Their joys, labors, trials, and hopes are the same. Their hearts beat against each other, and beat to the same time. This is a true union; it is such a union as God sanctions. These two classes of men and women should all be united. They would thus lay the foundation of a grand temple of love and harmony, the beauty and sweetness of which eye hath not seen, nor ear heard. There is also another class of women differing a little from the first, and a corresponding class of men, which should all be united. These might be called classes B. Then would follow other classes, till the whole race would be found to be properly associated in an almost innumerable number of classes or circles, one of male and another of female, throughout the whole series. To be properly united, each one of any class should be united with one of the corresponding class. If this could be universal, the race would be in harmony.

Now, suppose a man of the class A marries a woman of the class B. There must be a certain degree of inharmony existing between their natures, and a corresponding amount of unhappiness in their lives. If a man of the class A marries a woman of the class C, there will be a still greater amount of inharmony and unhappiness. And so on to the end of the chapter. The greater the difference in their natures, the greater the inharmony and unhappiness. This is the simple philosophy of marriage. Now, the question is, how shall we know our mates?—how shall we know the persons in the other sex which belong to the class of being that corresponds to our own?

We readily admit that this question is not so easily solved as many others. But still, with proper care, reflection, and honesty on the part of both men and women, it may be so solved that mistakes need seldom occur among the enlightened for whom I write.

I. First, it is necessary for the youth of both sexes to be perfectly *honest* in their intercourse with each other, so as to exhibit always their true character and nature. Dishonesty is, perhaps, a greater barrier even than ignorance to a proper understanding of the real character of those with whom we contemplate matrimonial alliances. Young men and women are not true to themselves. They put on false characters. They assume airs not their own. They shine in borrowed plumes. They practice every species of deception for the concealment of their real characters. They study to appear better than they are. They seek, by the adornments of dress and gems, by the blandishments of art and manner, by the allurements of smiles and honeyed words, by the fascination of pleasure and scenes of excitement, to add unreal, unpossessed charms to their persons and characters. They appear in each others' society to be the embodiment of goodness and sweetness, the personification of lofty principle and holy love, when, in fact, they are full of human weaknesses and frailties.

Now all these outward adornments and blandishments, which are not in accordance with, or the proper emblems of, the inward nature and character, are so many lies told to deceive somebody into a false and wicked alliance of marriage. When young people are thus deceitful with each other before marriage, it is only just and right that they should suffer after for their wickedness. It is the just penalty of their sin. Their lives ought to be as miserable after as they have been deceitful before marriage. And I believe they generally are. Another species of dishonesty, is in the objects for which people marry. The real object of marriage is companionship. But thousands marry for a home, for standing, for money, for passion, without telling their partners that these are their objects. Such marriages are most lying frauds, base forgeries of truth, that ought to be punished with their legitimate infelicity and wretchedness. Any man or woman that will deceive an intended companion with respect to the object of marriage, is too mean to have a good companion, or to enjoy one if in his or her possession. Now that wealth and cast exert so great an influence in the world, the honest marriages have become few. What man or woman proclaims among his or her associates that station or wealth is the object for which he or she desires a matrimonial alliance? And yet, how largely these things enter into the calculations of thousands of the unmarried! Now, all these calculations are dishonest, unless they are candidly expressed; for the real and implied object of marriage is companionship.

Whoever then, would make an intelligent choice of a

proper companion must be *honest*, and must commune with *honest* associates in the opposite sex. To be honest, one must act himself, be true to his interior man, make his outward life a meet expression of his inward. Thus he will be known to be just what he is. Every one has a natural intuition of kindredness, which will be an almost infallible guide when he and his associates are truly honest. But when one is under the influence of passion, or any false or wicked motive, his intuitive judgment is overwhelmed by the blinding power of that falsity, and is rendered wholly incapable of a correct decision, or of pure impressions. A dishonest man can neither trust his judgment or his impressions. They are more likely to be false than true.

Then, first of all, let youth be honest in their intercourse with each other. Thus they can know and be known, see and be seen as they really are; and natural companions will know each other almost as soon as they meet. Souls of real kindred make feel that kindredness almost as soon as they come into each other's presence, when they associate with pure hearts and honest purposes. They give each other an impression of congeniality which is pleasing and vivid, and may be considered as the instinctive indication of an internal companionship.

II. The second subject of interest and importance in our observations concerning a choice of a companion, is the physical constitution and temperament. We want a companion kindred with our own souls. The character of the soul is, to a certain extent, exhibited in the outward person. A coarse, harsh, roughly organized body is never the tabernacle of a refined, sensitive, and ardent spirit; nor is a refined, delicate, physical organism the dwelling-place of a dull, stupid, unfeeling, and harsh-toned soul. There is an exact and universal correspondence between the inward and outward man. This correspondence should be studied. Harmony of spirit will always be found connected with harmony of physical constitution, with respect to temperament. If we know our own temperament, our own degree of physical activity and refinement, we may find its correspondent for our companion. We shall thus secure physical harmony, thus secure the dulcet charm of physical kindredness. This is absolutely necessary to a full spiritual congeniality.

If our temperament is upon the extreme of coarseness or refinement, or upon any extreme, it is better for posterity that we choose a companion with a temperament less in the extreme than our own. However, it should always be marked with our own peculiarity. If one has very red or very light hair, it is better for his companion to have darker hair, or even black hair, with about the same degree of activity and refinement. The same may be said of the eyes and the general complexion. This secures about the same degree of spiritual delicacy and earnestness in the companions, and guards their posterity against extremes of temperament and character. Their influence is also favorable upon each other, gradually bringing back the character from the extreme. This, however, does not in the least favor the idea that those of an opposite character should marry. No greater error was ever inculcated.

Sometimes, however, an individual may be benefited who has some very bad or extreme trait of character by having a companion who is the reverse upon this point. But then the good one has to be made a martyr to the bad one, which is a kind of injustice not pleasant to be endured. People seeking companionship are not willing, as a general thing, to voluntarily become literally personal sacrifices to improve the character of a contemplated companion. Then seek for harmony of physical constitution and temperament, as absolutely necessary to congeniality of spirit.

III. The next point of importance is intellectual harmony. The intellectual characters of companions should be harmonious, and of about the same degree of strength. For a philosopher to marry a ninny, is absolutely wicked. For a genius to marry a blockhead, is suicidal to happiness. For a man of highly-cultivated intellect to companion with a woman of narrow and untutored mind, is no better, and "*vice versa.*" Intellectual enjoyments constitute a great portion of the real pleasure of life. They are solid, enduring, and satisfying. It is by the wisdom of intellect that we are guided in all our business concerns, philanthropic movements, and pleasure-seeking operations. Intellect is our pilot across the sea of life. A true and proper respect for one as a companion can not long be retained under a consciousness of that companion's inferiority. It is an equal we respect as we should a companion. It is impossible properly to respect an inferior. Let every youth, then, bear this in mind: an equal in intellectual endowment and cultivation should be a real companion.

IV. A harmony in *moral character* and *feeling* is absolutely essential to a full kindredness. In no respect is congeniality more important than in this. In the moral nature all the virtues have their birth. This is the Lord's garden. Here are philanthropy, religion, and faith. Here are hope and duty. Without harmony here there can be no permanent happiness. Marriage should be consecrated in this region of the mind. A difference of moral strength and activity, a difference in the sentiments of duty and goodness, a difference in the religious opinions and feelings, will constantly mar, or, at least, detract from the peace and happiness of any union, however perfect in other respects. Above all things else, seek for moral harmony of soul, seek for kindredness in this highest department of mind. Most sacred of all things are the sentiments here cherished. A union must extend to the moral nature, or it can not be true and blessed.

V. Equally important is a harmony of affection. The various affections of the heart should be mutually and equally cherished. A full, perfect, and ardent congeniality should be felt in all the loves. Home, country, friends, children, parents, and companion should be loved by companions with an equal ardor of soul. The charm of congenial love has been the theme of the orator, the divine, and the poet since Adam's union with Eve. Without a deep and earnest mutuality in love no two should ever be married. It is love that inspires and sanctions marriage. To indulge in the privileges of matrimony without love is a species of unparalleled sinfulness. It is love that hallows and makes them virtuous by its divine consecration. In order that love may be permanently mutual, there must be a general congeniality of nature, spirit, and character. The thoughts, opinions, feelings, activities, and pleasures must be mutual. Then love assumes its highest aspect; is placed upon its only sure foundation; and glows with its native ardor, to fill the soul with its unutterable charm of charms.

A proper attention to these several particulars, in a careful and sincere study of the whole character, under the lights of the various sciences which treat of human character and life, will enable one to determine with accuracy and confidence whether any individual is truly congenial with himself. This, however, is more than a brief study of a few days or weeks. It is the study of years. It is hazardous in the extreme to marry short of two or three years' acquaintance and careful study of the character of the contemplated companion. Not in a few brief interviews can the character of an individual be fully learned, or a full congeniality be discovered. Congenial spirits will more frequently be found in the walks of life and the circles of society in which we have been accustomed to move than elsewhere. Let youth be truly intelligent, sincere, and devout in the practical as well as theatrical pursuit of this subject, and almost sure will they be of securing to themselves the rich pleasures and inestimable benefits of this great institution ordained of Heaven, for human virtue, happiness, and exaltation in spirit.

A LIST OF WORKS

By Fowlers and Wells, Clinton Hall, 131 Nassau Street, New York.

In order to accommodate "The People," residing in all parts of the United States, the undersigned Publishers will forward by return of the First Mail, any book named in the following List. The postage will be pre-paid by them, at the New York Office. By this arrangement of pre-paying postage in advance, fifty per cent. is saved to the purchaser. The price of each work, including postage, is given, so that the exact amount may be remitted. All letters containing orders, should be post-paid, and directed as follows: FOWLERS AND WELLS, Clinton Hall, 131 Nassau Street, New York.

On Phrenology.

Combe's Lectures on Phrenology. A complete course. Bound in Muslin, $1 25.

Chart, for Recording various velopments. Designed for Phrenologists. 6 cents.

Constitution of Man. By Geo. Combe. Authorized Edition. Paper, 62 cts. Muslin, 87 cts.

Constitution of Man. School Edition. Arranged with Questions. 30 cents.

Defence of Phrenology, with Arguments and Testimony. By Dr. Boardman. Paper, 62 cents. Muslin, 87 cents.

Domestic Life, Thoughts on. Its Concord and Discord. By N. Sizer. 15 cents.

Education Complete. Embracing Physiology. Animal and Mental, Self-Culture, and Memory. In 1 vol. By O. S. Fowler. $2 50.

Education, Founded on the Nature of Man. Dr. Spurzheim. 62 cts. Muslin, 87 cts.

Familiar Lessons on Phrenology and Physiology. Muslin, in one volume. $1 25.

Love and Parentage: applied to the Improvement of Offspring. 30 cents. The same, in Muslin, including Amativeness. 75 cents.

Marriage: Its History and Philosophy. with Directions for Happy Marriages. Bound in Paper, 50 cents. Muslin 75 cents.

Memory and Intellectual Improvement: Applied to Self-Education. By O. S. Fowler. Paper, 62 cents. Muslin, 87 cents.

Mental Science, Lectures on, According to the Philosophy of Phrenology. By Rev. G. S. Weaver. Paper, 62 cents. Muslin, 87 cents.

Matrimony: or, Phrenology and Physiology applied to the Selection of Congenial Companions for Life. 30 cents.

Moral and Intellectual Science. By Combe, Gregory, and others. Muslin, $2 30.

Phrenology Proved, Illustrated, and Applied. Thirty-seventh edition. A standard work on the science. Muslin, $1 25.

Phrenological Journal, American Monthly. Quarto, Illustrated. A year, One Dollar.

Popular Phrenology, with Phrenological Developments. 30 cents.

Phrenology and the Scriptures. By Rev. John Pierpont. 12 cents.

Phrenological Guide: Designed for the Use of Students. 15 cents.

Phrenological Almanac: Illustrated with numerous engravings. 6 cents.

Phrenological Bust: designed especially for Learners, showing the exact location of all the Organs of the Brain fully developed. Price, including box for packing, $1 25. [Not mailable.]

Religion, Natural and Revealed, Or the Natural Theology and Moral Bearings of Phrenology. Paper, 62 cents. Muslin, 87 cents.

Self-Culture and Perfection of Character. Paper, 62 cents. Muslin, 87 cents.

Self-Instructor in Phrenology and Physiology, Illustrated, with One hundred Engravings. Paper, 30 cents. Muslin, 50 cents.

Synopsis of Phrenology and Physiology. By L. N. Fowler. 15 cents.

Symbolical Head and Phrenological Chart, in Map Form, showing the Natural Language of the Phrenological Organs. 25 cents.

Temperance and Tight-Lacing. On the Laws of Life. By O. S. F. 15 cents.

Works of Gall, Combe, Spurzheim and Others, together with all works on Phrenology, for sale, wholesale and retail. Agents and Booksellers supplied, by Fowlers and Wells, New York.

Hydropathy, or Water-Cure.

"IF THE PEOPLE can be thoroughly indoctrinated in the general principles of HYDROPATHY, they will not err much, certainly not fatally, in their home application of the WATER-CURE APPLIANCES to the common disease of the day. If they can go a step further, and make themselves acquainted with the LAWS OF LIFE AND HEALTH, they will well nigh emancipate themselves from all need of doctors of any sort."—DR. TRALL, IN HYDROPATHY FOR THE PEOPLE.

Accidents and Emergencies. By Alfred Smee. Notes by Trall. Illustrated. 15 cents.

Bulwer, Forbes and Houghton on the Water Treatment. One large volume. $1 25.

Cook-Book, Hydropathic. With new Recipes. By R. T. Trall, M. D. Paper, 62 cents. Muslin, 87 cents.

Children; Their Hydropathic Management in Health and Disease. By Dr. Shew. $1 25.

Consumption: Its Causes, Prevention and Cure. Paper, 62 cents. Muslin, 87 cents.

Curiosities of Common Water. A Medical work. From London edition. 30 cents.

Cholera: Its Causes, Prevention and Cure: and all other Bowel Complaints. 30 cts.

Confessions and Observations of a Water Patient. By Sir E. Lytton Bulwer. 15 cts.

Errors of Physicians and Others, in the Application of the Water-Cure. 30 cents.

Experience in Water-Cure, in Acute and other Diseases. By Mrs. Nichols. 30 cents.

Hydropathic Encyclopedia. A Complete System of Hydropathy and Hygiene. Illustrated. By R. T. TRALL, M. D. Two volumes, with nearly One Thousand pages. Illustrated. Price, $3 00.

Hydropathy for the People. Notes, by Dr. Trall. Paper, 62 cents. Muslin, 87 cents.

Hydropathy, or Water-Cure. Principles, and Modes of Treatment. Dr. Shew. $1 25.

Home Treatment for Sexual Abuses, with Hydropathic Management. A Practical Treatise for Both Sexes. By Dr. Trall. 30 cents.

Hygiene and Hydropathy, Lectures on. By R. S. Houghton, M. D. 30 cents.

Introduction to the Water-Cure. With First Principles. 15 cents.

Midwifery and the Diseases of Women. A practical work. By Dr. Shew. $1 25.

Milk Trade in New York and Vicinity. By Mullaly. Introduction by Trall. 30 cents.

Parent's Guide and Childbirth Made Easy. By Mrs. H. Pendleton. 60 cents.

Philosophy of Water-Cure. By John Balbirnie, M. D. A work for beginners. 30 cts.

Pregnancy and Childbirth, Water-Cure for Women, with cases. 30 cents.

Principles of Hydropathy; Invalid's Guide to Health. By D. A. Harsha. 15 cents.

Practice of Water-Cure. By Drs. Wilson and Gully. A handy, popular work. 30 cts.

Science of Swimming: Giving Practical Instruction to Learners. 12 cents.

Water-Cure Library; Embracing the Most Important Works on the Subject. In seven large 12mo. volumes. A Family work. $6 00.

Water-Cure in America, containing Reports of Three Hundred Cases. $1 25.

Water and Vegetable Diet in Scrofula, Cancer, Asthma, &c. By Dr. Lamb. Notes by Shew. 62 cents. Muslin, 87 cents.

Water-Cure in Every Known Disease. By J. H. Rausse. 62 cents. Muslin, 87 cents.

Water-Cure Manual; A Popular Work on Hydropathy. 62 cents. Muslin, 87 cents.

Water-Cure Almanac, Containing much important matter for all classes. 6 cents.

Water-Cure Journal and Herald of Reforms. Devoted to Hydropathy and Medical Reform. Published monthly, at One Dollar a Year.

FOWLERS AND WELLS have all works on PHYSIOLOGY, HYDROPATHY, and the Natural Sciences generally. Booksellers supplied on the most liberal terms. AGENTS wanted in every state, county, and town. These works are universally popular, and thousands might be sold where they have never yet been introduced.

TO PREVENT MISCARRIAGES, DELAYS OR OMISSIONS, all letters and other communications should, in ALL CASES, be post-paid, and directed to the Publishers, as follows:—FOWLERS AND WELLS, Clinton Hall, 131 Nassau St., New York.

Phonography and Miscellaneous.

When single copies of these works are wanted, the amount, in postage stamps, small change, or bank notes **may be enclosed** in a letter and sent to the Publishers, who will forward the books by return of the FIRST MAIL.

ON PHONOGRAPHY.

Constitution of the United States, in Phonography, Corresponding style. 15 cents.

Declaration of Independence, in Phonography, a sheet; for framing. 15 cents.

Phonographic Teacher; Being an Inductive Exposition of Phonography, intended for a school book, and to afford complete instruction to those who have not the assistance of an oral teacher. By E. Webster. In Boards. 45 cents.

Phonographic Envelopes, Large and Small, containing Brief Explanations of Phonography and its Utility. Price, per thousand, $3 25.

Phonographic Alphabet, upon Enamelled Card. Price, per hundred, $3 00.

Phonographic Word-Signs, on Card. Per hundred copies, $3 00.

The Universal Phonographer: Monthly Journal, devoted to the Dissemination of Phonography, and to Verbatim Reporting, with Practical Instruction to Learners. Printed in Phonography. [No discount on this work.] Price, A YEAR, $1 00.

MISCELLANEOUS.

Botany for all Classes; Containing a Floral Dictionary, with numerous Illustrations. Paper, 62 cents. Muslin, 87 cents.

Chemistry, Applied to Physiology, Agriculture, and Commerce. By Liebig. 25 cts.

Delia's Doctors; or, A Glance Behind the Scenes. By Miss Hanna Gardner Creamer. Paper, 62 cents. Muslin, 87 cents.

Essay on Wages, Showing the Necessity of a Workingman's Tariff. 15 cents.

Familiar Lessons on Astronomy. Designed for Children and Youth in Schools and Families. Mrs. Fowler. Paper, 62 cts. Muslin, 87 cts.

Future of Nations, A Lecture. By Louis Kossuth. Revised by the author. 12 cents.

Hints toward Reforms, in Lectures, Addresses, and other Writings. By H. Greeley. Second Edition, Enlarged, with Crystal Palace. $1 25.

Hopes and Helps for the Young of Both Sexes. By Rev. G. S. Weaver. An excellent work. Paper, 62 cents. Muslin, 87 cents.

Human Rights, and their Political Guaranties. By Judge Hurlbut. An important work. Paper, 62 cents. Muslin, 87 cents.

Home for All: New, Cheap, Convenient, and Superior Mode of Building. 87 cents.

Immortality Triumphant The Existence of a God, with the Evidence. By Rev. J. B. Dods. Paper, 62 cents. Muslin, 87 cents.

Innovation Entitled to a Full and Candid Hearing. By John Patterson. 15 cents.

Literature and Art. By S. Margaret Fuller. Introduction by Horace Greeley. $1 25.

Labor: Its History and Prospects. Use and Abuse of Wealth. By Owen. 30 cents.

Power of Kindness; Inculcating the Christian Principles of Love over Physical Force. Paper 30 cents. Muslin, 50 cents.

Population, Theory of. The Law of Animal Fertility. Introduction by Trall. 15 cts.

Temperance Reformation— Its History from the First Temperance Society to the Adoption of the Maine Law. By Armstrong. $1 25.

The Student: A Monthly Magazine, Devoted to the Physical, Moral, and Intellectual Improvement of Youth. Amply Illustrated. Price, One Dollar a Year.

Woman: Her Education and Influence. With an Introduction by Mrs. C. M. Kirkland. Paper, 50 cents. Muslin, 87 cents.

Woman, in all Ages and Nations. An Authentic History, from the Earliest Ages. Paper, 62 cents. Muslin, 87 cents.

THESE works may be ordered in large or small quantities. A liberal discount will be made to AGENTS, and others, who buy to sell again. They may be sent by Express or as Freight, by Railroad, Steamships, Sailing Vessels, by Stage or Canal, to any City, Town, or Village in the United States, the Canadas, to Europe, or any place on the Globe.

Checks or drafts, for large amounts, on New York, Philadelphia, or Boston, always preferred. We pay cost of exchange.

☞ All letters should be post-paid, and addressed as follows:— FOWLERS AND WELLS,

[Name the Post Office, Co., and State.] Clinton Hall, 131 Nassau St., New York.

www.ingramcontent.com/pod-product-compliance
Lightning Source LLC
LaVergne TN
LVHW050512100826
845148LV00002B/310

9781425521820